Strangled by Red Tape

A Heritage Foundation Collection of Regulatory Horror Stories

By Craig E. Richardson and Geoff C. Ziebart

The Heritage Foundation

Craig E. Richardson and Geoff C. Ziebart operate Richardson Ziebart Consulting in Arlington, Virginia.

Susan M. Eckerly, Deputy Director of Domestic Policy Studies at The Heritage Foundation during the preparation of this volume, has joined Citizens for a Sound Economy.

Robert E. Moffit is Deputy Director of Domestic Policy Studies at The Heritage Foundation.

Daniel Oliver is a Distinguished Fellow at The Heritage Foundation.

John Shanahan is a Heritage Foundation Policy Analyst specializing in environmental issues.

Adam D. Thierer is the Alex C. Walker Fellow in Economic Policy at The Heritage Foundation.

Note: The footnote documentation from the first edition of **Strangled by Red Tape** has been omitted in this special condensed edition.

To obtain a copy of the first edition, contact The Heritage Foundation at 202-546-4400 or write them at:

The Heritage Foundation
214 Massachusetts Avenue, NE
Washington, DC 20002.
ISBN 0-89195-059-1

Produced for The Heritage Foundation
by Jameson Books, Inc., Ottawa, IL.
815-434-7905
Printed in the United States of America
First printing, April 1995
5 4 3 2 1 97 96 95

Federal Regulations are —
Ridiculous
Expensive
Life-Threatening

That's the conclusion you'll come to after reading this Heritage Foundation collection of "horror stories" from your government in Washington, D.C.

Ridiculous? "Protecting the ozone and arresting global warming is so important to the [EPA] it is even researching the impact of cow belches and flatulence on global warming."

Expensive? ". . . efforts to save the Spotted Owl have cost 30,000 jobs and reduced lumber harvests. The cost of building a 2,000-square-foot house has increased by at least $4,000 since 1992."

Life-Threatening? ". . . physicians estimate that during the FDA's nine-year ban on beta blockers, a treatment for heart attacks, as many as 50,000 people died who might have been saved by the drug."

Contents

Preface

The message the American people sent to their Imperial Congress in November 1994 was a simple one: "We've had enough." The momentum from that victory, we can hope, may move the public next to demand saner—and fewer—regulations from our (unelected) Imperial Bureaucracies. If so, the second victory will perhaps be due in part to efforts like this Heritage Foundation book of regulatory "horror stories."

Everyone has a favorite story about over-regulation. Whether the offending bureaucracy is the FDA, the EPA, the IRS, Interior Department, OSHA, or EEOC, we at The Heritage Foundation have been observing and recording some of the most egregious examples of this governmental tyranny (or just plain absurdity) for some time now.

Life-threatening delays: "I see patients wrestle with [the FDA drug approval process] all the time," said Eugene Schonfeld, president of the National Kidney Cancer Association, who himself has kidney cancer. "I see some of them give up and say, 'OK, I can't fight it anymore. I'm going to die.' They have to fight the disease. That's bad enough. But to have to fight the bureaucracy is intolerable."

Absurd policy interpretations: Employees of DeBest Inc., a plumbing company, were working at a construction site in Garden City, Idaho, when they heard a backhoe operator yell for help. Two of the men jumped into the trench and dug the victim out, quite possibly saving his life. OSHA fined DeBest Inc. $7,875, claiming that the two men should not have gone into the trench without (1) putting on approved hard hats, and (2) taking steps to ensure that other trench walls did not collapse, and water did not seep in (while the victim simply suffocated?).

The costs to our overall economy and to individual lives in these cases are difficult to measure but easy to see and describe, precisely as we've done here.

And as we've stated in previous publications, our goal with this book is to help show the way to the fundamental systemic change necessary for the future health of our society.

EDWIN J. FEULNER, JR.
PRESIDENT
THE HERITAGE FOUNDATION

1

Reality Check: What Government Regulations Are Costing Us

Here's a short list of questions and answers about your government that may surprise—and appall—you . . .

Q. How much is each American household spending annually on Federal regulations?

A. **About $4,000 per year!** That's the all-in estimate from Thomas Hopkins, an economics professor at the Rochester Institute of Technology and former deputy administrator of OMB [Office of Management and Budget], based on a national expenditure of roughly $400 billion a year. Ron Utt, a former OMB official, estimates the cost may be greater, as much as $500 billion, or $5,000 per household. That comes to a 14 percent reduction in standard of living on the average household income of $32,000 (Doug

1

Bandow, Citizens Against Government Waste *Issue Brief* No. 8, Oct. 1993).

Q. What's the real-world impact of that reduction on our standard of living?

A. If American households are, on average, $4,000 poorer, that is $4,000 less they have to spend on consumer goods that enhance their health and safety. That **all tremendously expensive regulations may inhibit the ability of families and individuals to build healthier and wealthier lives** is the regulatory establishment's dirty little secret (*Washington Times*, June 3, 1992).

Q. How long does each American have to work each tax year in order to pay for this level of regulation?

A. According to the Americans for Tax Reform Foundation, it is not until May 5 each year that Americans have finished paying for all government spending. **But when the costs of regulations are taken into account, "each American is found to be working until July 10, over half the year, to pay for the total cost of government"** (Rep. Dick Armey, R-TX, *The Freedom and Fairness Restoration Act*, p. 21).

Q. What percent of this country's annual GNP is this Federal burden?

A. In 1990, the Federal government spent $1.251 trillion, **23.2 percent of GNP**. Regulation, at about $430 billion in 1990 dollars, raised that burden by more than one-third, making the real Federal share of the nation's economy **more than 30 percent** (Bandow, "Government Waste and the Terrible Ten," p. 10).

Q. Does this burden have an impact on new job creation?

A. Definitely. There are at least **three million fewer jobs in the American economy today** than would have existed if the growth of regulation over the last twenty years had been slower and regulations more efficiently designed (William G. Laffer III, Heritage Foundation *Backgrounder* No. 926, Feb. 16, 1993).

Q. What is the impact on manufacturing costs, for example?

A. To take only two examples, regulations add as much as 33 percent to the cost of building an airplane engine and as much as 95 percent to the price of a new vaccine" (IPI *Policy Report* No. 121, Feb. 1993).

Q. How about their impact on the tax base?

A. Regulations reduce the rate of return on investments made in the United States and encourage firms to move overseas. . . . Regulation discourages investment in the development of new technologies, manufacturing processes, and product designs . . . Large firms generally can absorb the cost of complying with regulatory programs more easily than smaller firms. Small and medium-sized firms find it more difficult to afford the high overhead costs of processing paperwork, paying attorney and accountant fees, and committing staff time to negotiating the federal regulatory maze . . . By reducing overall economic growth, **regulation shrinks the tax base** and reduces the amount collected by every specific tax (William G. Laffer III and Nancy A. Bord, Heritage Foundation *Backgrounder* No. 905, July 10, 1992).

Q. Can we guess which professional group has seen job growth during this period?

A. You probably can. The explosion in rules and regulations has paralleled an explosion in the number of attorneys in the United States. **"The number of lawyers has risen 250 percent since 1970,** to 1.24 million, and the Labor Department predicts the number could leap between 7 percent and 23 percent in the next 11 years"** (*Detroit News,* Aug. 9, 1994).

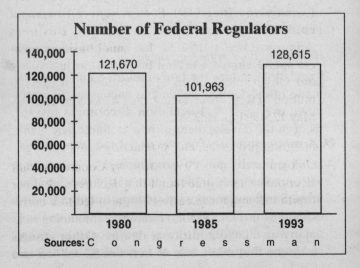

Number of Federal Regulators

1980	1985	1993
121,670	101,963	128,615

Sources: Congressman

Q. How much time do we business people spend annually dealing with these regulations?

A. A typical American business must fulfill provisions of the Clean Air and Clean Water Acts, provide a minimum standard of living for workers, engage in recycling, carry an expensive insurance policy against product liability, ferret out illegal aliens, provide costly packages of medical benefits to employees (these may have to include acupuncture, wigs, pastoral services, and drug treatment). They have to provide special accommodations to disabled employees and promote equal opportunity as determined by race, sex, and sexual activity. As Rep. Tom Delay points out, "There will be 100 forms and booklets of information that a typical business has to sort through and fill out to comply with Federal rules and regulations . . . The Small Business Administration estimated that **small business owners spend almost a billion hours a year** just filling out Government forms at an annual cost of $100 million" (Rep. Tom Delay, R-TX, *Congr. Record,* May 12, 1994, p. H3335).

Q. Are the costs to us taxpayers only financial in nature?

A. Unfortunately, no. A 1984 study by Congress's Joint Economic Committee found that declines in real per capita income in the early 1970s also led to a corresponding increase in total mortality, amounting to as many as 60,000 additional deaths. **Other studies estimate that every loss of between $3 million and**

$8 million to the economy will result in a premature death. This means that when the economy sours, people die. Therefore, regulations that depress the economy—for whatever reason—can have a deadly impact . . . Consider that current estimates place the annual regulatory burden on the economy as high as $400 billion to $500 billion. Assuming the same regulatory cost/premature death ratio cited above, this would mean **federal regulations are responsible for 40,000 to 50,000 premature deaths each year.** It should also be no surprise that the vast majority of these deaths would occur in financially strapped communities, such as South Central Los Angeles, where there is less institutional ability to compensate for economic losses (*Washington Times,* op. cit.).

Q. What does this kind of "net-benefit" analysis do to the arguments for all this regulation?

A. Making the conservative assumption that there is a premature death for every $10 million lost to the economy, many regulations would not pass muster with 'net-benefit' analysis, even granting the agencies their questionable assessments of their regulations' benefits and costs. Regulations that are unduly expensive range from the $13.5 million-per-premature-death-averted rule governing emissions of arsenic from glass plants to **a $5.7 trillion-per-premature-death-averted regulation covering wood preserving chemicals** [see chart below]. Under a 'net-benefit' analysis, most of these would be overturned. It is no wonder that the regulatory zealots are so upset. Should 'net-benefit' analysis ever be enshrined at OMB, it would curtail the ability to regulate (ibid.).

Costs Imposed by Selected Federal Regulations

Regulation	Agency	Year Enacted	Cost per Premature Death Averted
(1990 dollars)			
Arsenic emission standards for glass plants	EPA	1986	$13.5 million
Ethylene oxide occupational exposure limit	OSHA	1984	$20.5 million
Hazardous waste listing for petroleum mining sludge	EPA	1990	$27.6 million
Dichloropropane drinking water standard	EPA	1991	$653 million
Formaldehyde occupational exposure limit	OSHA	1987	$82.202 billion
Atraxine/alachor drinking water standard	EPA	1991	$92.07 billion

Q. What's the impact of all this on small business?

A. Federal government regulations enacted since 1989 have imposed significant burdens on small business, stifling job creation and causing a decline in real wages, according to a report released November 7, 1992 by Rep. Richard Armey (R-TX) ... The report cited 1989 amendments to the Fair Labor Standards Act raising the minimum wage, the Americans with Disabilities Act, the Civil Rights Act of 1991, and the Clean Air Act Amendments of 1990 as among the "spate of burdensome new regulations which could hardly have been better designed to thwart small business job creation." **These laws make up the bulk of a 34.4 percent increase in the government's burden on small business since 1989,** the report said (Bureau of National Affairs *Daily Report* ... , Nov. 9, 1992).

Q. A 'e business people aware of this situation?

A. Increasingly so. "Government regulations are the biggest challenge to middle-market companies and frequently demand considerable time from the company owner or president, according to a recent telephone poll conducted by Arthur Andersen's Enterprise Group. **More than half of those polled, 52 percent, named government regulation as the most challenging issues [sic] facing mid-sized businesses, outranking health care and insurance issues considered most challenging by 20 percent** ... Of all regulations, environmental rules are the 'greatest burden' to mid-sized business, according to 40 percent of poll participants. Twenty-four percent note OSHA regulations as a burden and 16 percent cite

federal income tax regulations as most burdensome"
(*Business Wire,* Mar. 14, 1994).

*Q. Can all this regulation really be called rational
behavior?*

A. One response: "At its best, the process makes no
sense, and at its worst, regulators classify their chil-
dren's teeth as toxic waste, they force banks to
make teller machines accessible to blind drivers,
they dictate that hard hats must be disinfected
before each use, and they require employers to
inform employees about the hazards of coming in
contact with Joy dishwashing liquid" (Rep. Tom
Delay, R-TX, *Congr. Record,* May 12, 1994,
p. H3334).

Q. In terms of verbiage, some comparisons, please—

A. Consider the following: "The Lord's Prayer is 66
words, the Gettysburg Address is 286 words, and
there are 1,322 words in the Declaration of Indepen-
dence. Yet, **government regulations on the sale of
cabbage total 26,911 words**" (Americans for Tax
Reform Foundation, "Cost of Government Day,"
Oct. 13, 1992).

Q. Has President Clinton recognized this situation?

A. Even President Bill Clinton, who many would argue
is responsible for instituting an era of increased regulation, criticizes the federal government: "This is a
report which says the whole way the government
operates is incompatible with the world in which

we're living, and we can change it. . . " (*Houston Chronicle,* Sept. 8, 1993)

Q. Have members of his administration made other statements suggesting a different view?

A. Yes. Example: "'Under my leadership, we are going to take—and already have taken—a much more aggressive approach to protecting consumers,' Ann Brown, chairman of the Consumer Product Safety Commission told *Investor's Business Daily.* Brown was formerly vice president of the Consumer Federation of America, a consumer activist group that often chastised Reagan and Bush officials for lax regulatory enforcement" (*Investor's Business Daily,* Apr. 19, 1994)

Q. An isolated incident?

A. Regrettably, no. *Investor's Business Daily* cites numerous other examples of a more aggressive federal government under Clinton: the "$50 billion a year" workplace safety bill pushed by Labor Secretary Robert Reich; the National Highway Traffic Safety Administration's "more aggressive" enforcement of auto safety standards, which resulted in "a 20% jump in auto-recall campaigns" in 1993; and the Administration's push for "more aggressive 'community reinvestment' requirements," which the American Bankers Association estimates "will add more than $150 million in administrative costs to the industry" (ibid.).

Q. Are there specific numbers that confirm this bias?

A. Yes. President Clinton's first year saw the most regulatory activity since President Carter's last. The page
total for 1993 of the *Federal Register* was 69,608
pages, the third highest total of all time. A not surprising increase in the number of regulatory bureaucrats corresponds with this proliferation of
regulation. While from 1988 to 1992 regulatory
staffing increased by over 20 percent to almost
125,000 employees, under President Clinton the
largest number of Federal bureaucrats ever, **128,615
people were called for to run his Federal regulatory
apparatus** (Delay, pp. H3334-H3335).

2

A Cure Worse Than the Illness?
(Food and Drug Administration)

Introduction by Robert E. Moffit

The Food and Drug Administration (FDA) is one of the Federal government's most powerful regulatory agencies. Operating as a division of the Public Health Service (PHS) within the huge U.S. Department of Health and Human Services (HHS), it has a staff of more than 9,000, including scientists and medical specialists, and a budget of $764 million. Its mission is consumer protection, and in recent years the scope of its regulatory authority has broadened dramatically. No other federal agency affects the lives of Americans more directly than the FDA. According to its own estimate, **Americans spend 25 cents out of every dollar on FDA-regulated products.** These products range from sophisticated prescription drugs, biologics, and medical devices to cosmetics, color television sets, and domestic and imported foods.

Most of the FDA's work—approximately 90 percent—involves enforcement of the Federal Food, Drug, and Cosmetic Act of 1938, from which the FDA derives the authority to regulate food (including imported food), human and animal drugs, medical devices, and cosmetics. Its consumer protection function includes pre-market approval and quality standards for drugs and medical devices, factory inspections, and market surveillance. It can combat such transgressions as the mislabeling of drugs or the adulteration of foods by seizing products and taking them off the market, by recommending **criminal prosecution** of violators to the Department of Justice, or by seeking **injunctions in Federal courts** against producers who manufacture or ship products not meeting legal or regulatory standards of consumer safety.

With respect to pharmaceuticals, Congress expanded the FDA's authority even further with the Drug Amendments of 1962, which provided that before a drug may be marketed, it must be shown to be effective as well as safe. With passage of the Medical Device Amendments of 1976, Congress similarly expanded FDA's authority over medical (including diagnostic) devices.

To implement this broad mandate, the FDA pursues a variety of strategies. It imposes safety and effectiveness standards on the manufacturing and testing of drugs and medical devices; monitors the food, drug, and cosmetics markets; conducts periodic inspections

and investigations; encourages recalls of products that
are deemed unsafe or ineffective; seeks Justice Department criminal proceedings or requests injunctive relief
from the Federal courts; or simply issues press releases.
Underlying everything else, however, is **coercive regulatory power:** the authority to set forth in meticulous
detail what companies must do to obtain permission to
market their products.

Most of the controversy surrounding the FDA
involves its drug approval process: laboratory and animal studies; three phases of clinical study, including
safety, effectiveness, and extensive clinical testing, fol-
lowed by agency review; and then final approval. All
told, it now takes approximately **twelve years to move a
drug from laboratory to market.** According to a 1993
study by Congress's Office of Technology Assessment,
the cost is about **$359 million per drug!**

In recent years, the FDA has come under increasing
criticism. Some critics, wondering whether the agency
has the institutional capacity to cope with rapid
advances in biomedical science, argue for streamlin-
ing its regulatory process. The heavy concentration
on research and development should be matched by a
change in the bureaucratic culture that contributes to
backlogs; in 1994, for example, there were 107 AIDS-
related medicines under development. Others, particularly liberals in Congress, think the agency does not
have enough enforcement authority. Michigan Demo-
crat John Dingell, for many years chairman of the
powerful House Energy and Commerce Committee,

thinks the already powerful agency should even be more independent (Robert Pear, *New York Times,* Apr. 11, 1991).

More and more policymakers, however, want to streamline or curtail the FDA's regulatory authority. AIDS activists have pressed for more expeditious review of AIDS-related drugs. Reagan administration officials established a requirement in 1981 that the FDA Commissioner get the approval of the Secretary of Health and Human Services before issuing regulations. During the Bush Administration, Vice President Dan Quayle's White House Competitiveness Council proposed expeditious approval of drugs to combat life-threatening diseases such as AIDS, cancer, and cystic fibrosis. Free-market economists have criticized proposals to expand FDA's enforcement authority, arguing that the agency's already cumbersome regulatory process, particularly for drugs, undermines the health of American citizens (Paul Rubin, Heritage Foundation *Backgrounder* No. 900, June 11, 1992).

• "The FDA makes its presence felt more widely than most Americans realize. The federal agency's oversight authority ranges over food, food additives, drugs and medical devices, TVs and microwave ovens. And pet products ... An estimated **25 cents of every dollar spent by consumers** falls within the FDA empire. It is often called the largest consumer protection agency in the world" (Peter Brimelow and Leslie Spencer, *Forbes,* Nov. 22, 1993, p. 115).

- "[The FDA] is deeply rooted in unlimited enthusi-
asm for government regulatory intervention, naive
confidence in legalistic processes and an unthinking
insensitivity as to means. And, of course, it provides
a very handy platform for publicity-hungry congress-
men. Characteristic statist symptoms exhibited by
the FDA:

   "Out-of-control expansion: The FDA has
   expanded remarkably since the 1960s. Total
   staff: now 9,000, up from 7,800 in 1990 and
   1,678 in 1960. It is constantly looking for new
   items to regulate as an excuse to get more
   money from Congress. FDA imperial ambitions
   in the pharmaceutical area go even beyond
   U.S. borders: Despite industry protest, it is
   working diplomatically to impose U.S.-type
   drug approval standards (invariably more strin-
   gent) on other countries.

   "Browbeating those subject to its jurisdiction:
   The FDA empire's drug company subjects whimper about its rule. A sample complaint: Any drug
   application is handled by several different people. Chronic lack of communication results in
   confusing and contradictory instructions.

   "Few, however, whimper very loudly . . . *Food &
   Drug Insider Report* . . . found that **84% of companies polled in 1991 reported declining to file a
   complaint against the FDA for fear of retalia-
   tion**" (ibid., pp. 115–116).

- "As is always the case with any Big Brother, he fears errors of commission, for which he can easily be blamed. But errors of omission, such as 'drug lag,' are hidden. 'They [FDA bureaucrats] don't have to prove anything. They can just say "I'm not sure, go do five more tests,"' says food and drug lawyer Peter Barton Hutt. '**The people who do premarket approval at FDA are like little kings and queens in their kingdom.** They can have more power over the economy and technological development than the chairman of the board of the largest pharmaceutical company'" (ibid., p. 118).

- "The number of workers at the Food and Drug Administration has grown from 4,470 in 1970 to 9,217—**a 106-percent increase**—and its budget (measured in 1987 dollars) has jumped from $227 million to

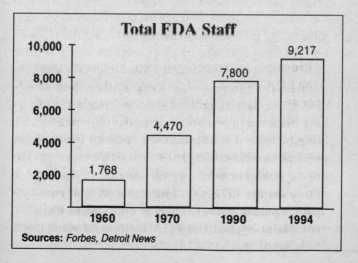

Total FDA Staff

1960	1970	1990	1994
1,768	4,470	7,800	9,217

Sources: *Forbes, Detroit News*

$764 million—**a 237-percent hike.** Today, FDA rules occupy 4,270 pages in the Code of Federal Regulations" (*Detroit News,* op. cit.).

Proving "Efficacy" or Just Unnecessary Delays?

Critics charge that having to prove a drug's efficacy in addition to its safety has severely slowed down approval time, created monumental regulatory hurdles, and effectively granted even greater bureaucratic powers to the FDA.

- "Prior to 1962, the FDA tested proposed new drugs solely to insure their safety. But since then, the FDA, on its own authority, has also demanded that drug manufacturers prove the efficacy of their products. This efficacy requirement and the manner of its enforcement has made it far more difficult for companies to get permission to provide new drugs to ailing Americans. Lawyer Sam Kazman of the Competitive Enterprise Institute noted, 'The 1962 law fundamentally changed the new drug approval process. Rather than simply evaluating data submitted by drug companies, FDA now became involved in drug development itself, bringing with it **a bureaucratic concern for avoiding politically embarrassing risks** even if this meant undermining public health.' Largely because of this shift, it now takes the FDA three times longer to review new drugs, and the number of new drugs approved each year has fallen by over 60 percent" (James Bovard, *Lost Rights,* St. Martin's Press, 1994, p. 62).

- "Charles Strother, a University of Wisconsin neurora-diologist, complained, 'Scientists and engineers are now using state-of-the-art techniques to create products to address previously incurable diseases and save lives, only to deliver them to an FDA still mired in the horse-and-buggy days of 10-year, double-blind trials.' The FDA has an extremely timid, risk-averse approach to approving new drugs; National Cancer Institute officials have accused the FDA of being '**mired in a 1960s philosophy of drug development, viewing all new agents as . . . poisons**'" (ibid., pp. 62–63).

- "[The Delaney Clause] mandates that prescription medicines cannot be made available until the FDA has certified not only their safety, but also their efficacy. As a result, tens of thousands of people have died unnecessarily while waiting for the heart-attack drugs streptokinase and TPA and the gastric-ulcer drug misoprostol. Alzheimer's sufferers and their families have been frustrated by the agency's refusal to authorize the use of the drug THA, despite evidence that it has helped four of ten patients who have tried it" (Bandow, "Regulatory Waste," p. 2).

FDA Approval: Time Consuming, Costly—Even Deadly?

- "A recent study by Tufts University's Center for the Study of Drug Development showed that 80% of drugs approved by the FDA between 1987 and 1989 were available earlier in other countries—by an average of about six years. With this delay, **the FDA was in effect killing Americans**" (Brimelow and Spencer, op. cit., p. 117).

- "It cost an average of $231 million to develop each drug approved during the 1980s, more than double the inflation-adjusted cost in the previous decade ... 'Most of that cost increase has been regulation driven,' says Leigh Thompson, chief scientific officer at Eli Lilly. He notes that in 1985, before drug approval applications were computerized, **one Lilly submission weighed 4,000 pounds and filled an entire room.** Since then, FDA data requirements have almost doubled" (ibid.).

- "On the average, development of a new drug takes about a decade and costs $231 million. In 1991, final FDA reviews alone had averaged 2-1/2 years. One drug for arthritis was approved last year after **nearly nine years under FDA review;** another for angina was reviewed by the agency for eight years" (Lochhead, "FDA Assailed for Slow Testing of New Drugs," p. A1).

- "[B]y 1967 FDA's average review time for new drug applications (NDAs) had more than quadrupled, from 7 to 30 months. **The average total development time for a new drug, which was five years in the early 1960s, is now a decade.** And whereas the U.S. was once a leader in pharmaceutical innovation, since the mid-1960s it has lagged behind Great Britain in new drug introductions" (S. Kazman, National Chamber Policy Analysis, "Saying Yes to Drugs," pp. 1-2).

- "[T]he FDA is currently incapable of giving approval to the release of new medical devices into the market-place. These devices at my company, Biomet, include such things as hip and knee replacements, bone screws, and bone healing products. In fact, the FDA has become such an impediment to the introduction of new devices in the United States that most new or improved devices are available to the rest of the world more than a year in advance of the U.S . . ." (D. Miller, Heritage Foundation Lecture No. 482, Dec. 8, 1993, pp. 1, 5).

Bureaucrats Making Life-and-Death Decisions

The evidence indicates that the FDA's slow bureau-cratic attitude may have contributed to the deaths of thousands of Americans. The agency seems to focus on less important issues like labeling while allowing badly needed medical devices and drugs to become bogged down in its protracted approval process.

- "Dubbed 'Lord of the Label' by the *Washington Post,* Mr. Kessler is responsible for the daring 1991 FDA raid that captured 24,000 half-gallons of Citrus Hill 'fresh choice' orange juice—all because the FDA control freaks didn't like the way the o.j. was labeled. Now they've decided to do us a favor by requiring food manufacturers to plaster government-approved content labels on all their products . . . Mr. Kessler

and company even have come up with the bureaucrats' definition of what's healthy and what's not . . .
[A]s the *Washington Post* put it: 'Webster's New
World Dictionary defines "healthy" in fewer than 20
words. The government definition will fill a page in
the Federal Register,' the official guide to Washington's rules and regulations" (Edwin J. Feulner, Jr.,
Washington Times, July 3, 1994).

- "Perhaps you have seen these novelty lollipops, which
  consist of a clear, tequila-flavored hard candy, inside
  of which is what appears to be a dead worm. If so, you
  no doubt asked yourself: 'What assurance do I have,
  as a consumer, that this worm is identified with proper
  federal terminology?' Rest easy! The FDA is on the
  case! According to the May 13, 1993, issue of *Food
  Labeling News,* the FDA sent a warning letter to S.S.
  Lollipop Co., manufacturers of the 'Sugar-Free Hotlix
  Tequila Flavored Candy With Genuine Worm,'
  because the company failed to properly identify the
  worm as an 'insect larva.' Not only THAT, but the
  FDA says that the product is NOT sugar-free" (Dave
  Barry, *Chicago Tribune Sunday Magazine,* Sept. 26,
  1993, p. 44).

The tragedy is that such seemingly frivolous bureaucratic pursuits can have **devastating consequences** for the
very citizens the FDA supposedly is trying to protect.

- "The FDA's power to approve or deny permission to
  use medical devices routinely gives its officials the
  power of life and death—a power that is often exer-

cised with bureaucratic negligence . . . FDA restrictions have made it almost impossible for physicians to use certain new medical devices without specific permission from an FDA official in Washington. A *Wall Street Journal* editorial entitled 'The FDA Meets A Patient' reported:

'"To the elites of Washington, medical regulation is an abstract "social good." To a 75-year-old woman from Portland, Maine, the not-so-abstract FDA is the regulator that this week nearly caused her to go blind. The woman was diagnosed some weeks ago to have an aneurysm the size of a golf ball in her cavernous carotid artery. Pressure built against her third cranial nerve until she could barely open her eyes. She risked blindness or rupture that could cause a stroke, yet the aneurysm's location made traditional brain surgery close to impossible. Dr. Eddie Kwan of Tufts University . . . proposed to use a device called a detachable silicone balloon . . . Tufts University, it turns out, isn't one of the 25 U.S. sites approved under newly restrictive FDA rules for use of the balloon (which is widely available outside the U.S). . . . But 75-year-olds with golf-ball sized aneurysms in danger of rupture aren't good candidates for travel. So Dr. Kwan proceeded to see if he could get permission through the bureaucratic politics at Commissioner David Kessler's FDA. 'The first time I talked to someone at the FDA, he just brushed me off,' says Dr. Kwan . . . 'I talked to so many people I can't remember their names.'"

"Kwan recruited other Tufts administrators to call the FDA to try to get permission; the callers were bounced around until they were instructed to file a formal request by fax. Tufts officials sent a fax explaining their case and pleading for immediate emergency approval—and heard nothing for four days. Finally, an FDA engineer with the illustrious title of 'branch chief for neurological devices' gave permission to Kwan to use the silicone balloon in an operation the following day. The operation saved the woman's eyesight and perhaps also her life. The *Wall Street Journal* observed:

"'One lesson . . . is that even the FDA can't face itself in the morning if forced to decide that a patient can't be treated. But what about all the other patients? What about patients who don't have a doctor or hospital willing to risk retribution by pestering the FDA? . . . **How is it that an obscure bureaucrat without a medical degree can become in effect the Chief of American Neuroradiology, with life-or-death decisions in his hands?**'" (Bovard, op. cit., pp. 63–64).

• Tacrine, "a drug developed in 1986 and widely available overseas to treat Alzheimer's symptoms," languished in the FDA approval process while approximately 4 million Americans suffering from the disease waited. "'**They [FDA bureaucrats] play God with us**,' said George Rhenquist, president of the Families for Alzheimer's Rights Association. Decisions about whether to prescribe drugs that are safe but not yet proven effective are better made by

patients and their doctors, not the FDA, he said. 'Why
should they have control over the lives of our loved
ones?'" (Lochhead, "FDA Assailed . . . ," p. A1).

- "In November 1987, FDA approved streptokinase as
  the first drug which could be intravenously adminis-
  tered to reopen the blocked coronary arteries of heart
  attack victims. Streptokinase had been shown to
  reduce in-hospital mortality among heart attack
  patients by 18 percent. In the U.S. approximately
  700,000 heart attack patients are hospitalized annually, of whom 9 percent die in-hospital. Thus, streptokinase could potentially save 11,000 of these lives each
  year" (Kazman, "Deadly Overcaution . . . ," p. 44).

- "[S]ome physicians estimate that during the FDA's
  nine-year ban on beta blockers, a treatment for heart
  attacks, **as many as 50,000 people died who might have
  been saved by the drug**" (Lochhead, op. cit., p. A4).

- "'I see patients wrestle with [the approval process] all
  the time,' said Eugene Schonfeld, president of the
  Chicago-based National Kidney Cancer Association,
  who himself has kidney cancer. 'I see some of them
  give up and say, "OK, I can't fight it anymore. I'm
  going to die." They have to fight the disease. That's
  bad enough. **But to have to fight the bureaucracy is
  intolerable**'" (Lochhead, op. cit., p. A1).

- "In the 3-1/2 years it took the FDA to approve the
  drug Interleukin 2, about 35,000 kidney cancer

patients died. The only known treatment for metastatic renal cell carcinoma, a fatal kidney cancer, had already been approved in nine European countries. The therapy is risky: The odds of being helped by the drug are about one in four, and the odds of dying from it are about one in 25. But the disease itself is always fatal" (ibid.).

• "With hundreds of thousands of Americans collapsing each year from sudden cardiac arrest, it is hard to believe that the government would halt testing of a treatment that nearly doubles their revival rate. But that is exactly what Food and Drug Administration regulators did this month—halting clinical testing of a simple but remarkable device that could mean the difference between life and death for millions of heart attack victims . . . One of FDA's chief arguments for halting the tests was that the doctors or emergency medical personnel did not obtain the consent of the patients in advance of using the device . . . Incredibly, FDA halted testing of the pumping device just as the hospital team researching its effectiveness planned to sign up 260 patients in an expanded study . . . The pump is being marketed and used throughout much of Europe as well as in Canada and Great Britain. Ambulances are required to carry it as part of their equipment in Austria. And it was approved for use in France after less than six months' evaluation. But not in America" (D. Lambro, *Washington Times*, May 19, 1994, p. A18).

• "[A]nother FDA policy that results in many deaths—
censorship of information about legal products—is
less widely recognized. The FDA prohibits unap-
proved health claims about the products it regulates,
including foods, nutrients, prescription drugs, over-
the-counter drugs, and medical devices. Instead of dis-
seminating important health information, the agency
actively suppresses it, causing hundreds of thousands
of premature deaths every year . . . [M]ore than a
dozen clinical trials since the late '40s have shown that
low-dose aspirin can significantly reduce the risk of
heart attack . . . These results are widely accepted
among doctors and scientists. Even so, the FDA has
specifically prohibited aspirin companies from men-
tioning this study in their advertising because preven-
tion of first heart attacks is not an FDA-approved
claim. Yet no pharmaceutical company is going to
undergo the huge expense of obtaining FDA approval
for a health claim about an unpatentable substance"
(D. Pearson and S. Shaw, *Reason,* vol. 24, no. 11
Apr. 1993, p. 52).

FDA Can Destroy Businesses

The FDA's regulatory power over food, drugs, and
medical devices means that the agency literally can
make or break those within its jurisdiction. While
larger companies may be able to withstand the
lengthy and costly approval process or the frequent
lawsuits, many smaller start-up companies can be
driven out of business.

- "A logjam at the Food and Drug Administration in approving medical devices is creating particular havoc at small companies. The backlog of requests to sell 510(k) devices—those 'substantially equivalent' to equipment already on the market—more than doubled to 3,950 last September from 1,900 two years earlier, and the number is growing, the FDA concedes. **The average review time has shot up to about 170 days from 98 in 1990** . . . *Biomedical Market Newsletter* mocks the agency with a 'Hall of Shame' list of recently approved products, including a disposable shoe cover that publisher David Anast says should never have been put through the regulatory treadmill" (B. Bowers, *Wall Street Journal,* June 4, 1993, p. B2).

- "While the agency [FDA] keeps many medical-device producers in limbo with long delays in approving new products, it can also take away approvals—often with devastating results. Critics say **the zeal of some FDA bureaucrats is crimping one of the most vibrant sectors of the U.S. economy.** The Health Industry Manufacturers Association says 11,000 U.S. companies produce close to half of the world's medical instruments. These companies' sales last year grew 8% from the previous year to $42.9 billion and their exports rose 8% to $9.7 billion, creating a $4.7 billion trade surplus in the category. Most of the device makers are small, which makes them particularly vulnerable in case of regulatory problems" (Bowers, *Wall Street Journal,* Apr. 12, 1994, p. B2).

- "Gene Oden could not have imagined how much his life would change when 20 Federal agents burst into his office in June 1993 and began seizing products crucial to his dietary supplement business. More than a year later the Food and Drug Administration has yet to file charges against Mr. Oden. Still **he has been forced to lay off all but 28 of his 105 employees while he wages war with the FDA hoping to recover more than $1 million in products the agents seized**" (Rep. John Duncan, R-TN, *Congr. Record,* July 28, 1994, p. H6437).

- "Physio-Control, a unit of pharmaceutical company Eli Lilly . . . is still reeling from its run-in with the [FDA]. Physio pioneered emergency defibrillators and is a leading producer of the devices, which are used to restore a normal heartbeat. But in May 1992, it stopped production of the electroshock devices at its factory in Redmond, Wash., after FDA inspectors questioned its production methods and record-keeping. President Richard Martin says the company signed a consent decree to stop shipments of its Lifepak 9, Lifepak 10 and Lifepak 300 defibrillators and devoted itself full time to addressing the FDA's concerns . . . [Martin] says the production stoppage has cost the company $70 million in 'out-of-pocket dollars to stay in business' and more than $100 million more in lost sales" (Bowers, op. cit.).

- "International Rehabilitative Sciences Inc., which does business as R S Medical, had FDA authorization to market its muscle stimulators. But in 1990, it sought clearance a second time to clarify its ownership of the products. The FDA denied the application—and rescinded its original clearance. Believing that it was being treated unfairly, the Vancouver, Wash., company tried an experiment. It applied again, twice: once under its own name, and separately under the name of a California consulting company that it hired to pose as a device maker. The consulting company got the approval without a hitch . . . R S Medical got another rejection. The company noted the discrepancy to the FDA, but the door was again slammed in its face, its lawyer says" (ibid.).

3

Hazardous to Our (Economic) Health?
(Environmental Protection Agency)

Introduction by John Shanahan

One of the most egregiously overzealous components of the Federal regulatory and enforcement apparatus is the Environmental Protection Agency (EPA). Formed in 1970 during the Nixon Administration to combat a real and growing pollution problem, the EPA unfortunately has been a classic example of **another cure that is worse than the disease.** In the name of environmental protection, it has imposed heavy-handed restrictions on businesses and individuals that are costly and that waste our nation's resources. Many of its enforcement actions have been insensitive, unreasonable, or intended to intimidate would-be violators. **It is now a felony to**

violate—even inadvertently—many regulations that are so complicated and ambiguous that even experts disagree on how to comply with them.

In the 1970s and early 1980s, the EPA focused on businesses. Industry was a chief cause of pollution, smokestacks are easy to identify, and the pace of cleanup was fairly rapid. Over the years, however, federal environmental laws and regulations generally have been inflexible, expensive, and at times unnecessary. **One of the most complicated, wasteful, illogical, and unfair is Superfund.** Passed in 1980, this law requires that a company (or a newspaper boy, for that matter) responsible for a small amount of pollution—say less than 1 percent of the total, perhaps because of a few car batteries thrown into a waste site—can be held liable for the entire cost of a multi-million-dollar cleanup. This program has cost the taxpayer $20 billion, yet only a small percentage of Superfund sites have been cleaned up because **the law encourages expensive litigation** more than it encourages cleanup.

The costs of complying with Superfund, the Clean Air Act, and other environmental laws in large part have been passed down to consumers in the form of higher prices. The only silver lining in the cloud used to be that these costs at least were spread among many companies and consumers. In the 1980s, this began to change. Since businesses had reduced pollution substantially and incremental reductions were becoming increasingly expensive, **the EPA turned its attention to small companies, entrepreneurs, and individuals.** The results have been disastrous. Small developers and retired couples, for example, have seen their savings destroyed when the EPA and Army Corps of Engineers classified their property as wetlands and off-limits to any construction. How much do these agencies pay when regulation effectively confiscates the land to preserve wetlands? Nothing! They claim payment is unnecessary because they are regulating for the "public good." The claim is specious. No public good ever came from institutionalizing government wrongs against law-abiding citizens.

This chapter explores many compelling examples of regulatory excess by the EPA and, in some cases, the Army Corps of Engineers. Unfortunately, far too many of these stories are as tragic as they are compelling.

A recent increase in public concern for the environment, coupled with the passage of enormously complex and far-reaching legislation like the Clean Air Act, has resulted in a tremendous accumulation of regulatory power within the U.S. Environmental Protection Agency. It is estimated conservatively that implementing environmental regulations costs the taxpayer **approximately $150 billion a year.** Much of this spending, like many of the costs imposed by other regulations, is unnecessary. But the available evidence also indicates that **Federal agencies have used the law in such areas as wetlands protection and Superfund to dictate how private property may and may not be used.** In some cases, American citizens have been bankrupted and/or jailed for environmental "crimes" allegedly committed on their own property.

The EPA is relatively new to the regulatory game compared to other federal agencies, but it clearly has caught-up in terms of size and reach.

- "The EPA now has 18,000 staff and an operating budget of $4.5 billion. That's about **a seventh of the staff and a third of the spending of the entire Federal regulatory apparatus.** The EPA's staff has quadrupled since 1970. Its inflation-adjusted spending has gone up ten times" (P. Brimelow and L. Spencer, Forbes, July 6, 1992).

Considering its tremendous resources, as well as its broad and ever-expanding regulatory authority, the magnitude of the agency's economic impact is hardly surprising.

- "[The EPA] reckons it has imposed some $1.4 trillion in compliance costs (1990 dollars) on industry since its founding in 1970 . . . In 1990 the agency estimated that complying with its pollution-control regulations was costing Americans $115 billion a year, or a remarkable 2.1% of GNP, versus 0.9% in 1972. (And critics complain EPA estimates are typically too low.) Put it this way: **Because of pollution controls, every American is paying on average about $450 more in taxes and higher prices. That's $1,800 for a family of four—about half its average expenditure on clothing and shoes.** In the 1990s the EPA projects that compliance costs will total another $1.6 trillion. And that's not counting the radical 1990 Clean Air Act amendments legislation. It could add $25 billion to $40 billion annually. Tellingly, the U.S. spends a larger share of its gross national product on pollution control than do most Western European countries. Yet they have far denser populations. France, for example, with 56 million people in rather less space than Texas, spends only two-thirds as much" (ibid.).

• "A 1990 study, by Michael Hazilla of American University and Raymond Kopp of Resources for the Future, looking mainly at the impact of the Clean Air Act and the Clean Water Act, found that real GNP was 6% lower than it otherwise would have been in 1990 due to these laws. Real consumption was 6.5% lower, real private domestic investment was more than 8% lower, and prices were more than 6% higher . . . According to a 1993 study from the National Bureau of Economic Research, environmental regulations reduce total factor productivity (that is, both labor and capital productivity) by three to four times the direct cost of the regulation. As a consequence, productivity (for the period 1979–85) was 3.1% lower in the oil industry, 5.3% lower in the paper industry and 7.6% lower in the steel industry than it would have otherwise been" (B. Bartlett, *Wall Street Journal,* Sept. 14, 1994).

Using the broad coercive powers available to it in such areas as clean water, wetlands protection, and Superfund, the Environmental Protection Agency has mounted a costly regulatory assault on businesses and individuals. The agency (unlike the Food and Drug Administration) may not be indirectly responsible for regulating Americans to death by denying them access to pharmaceuticals and new medical technology, but it has produced its share of regulatory horror stories—for example, by **placing people in jail for working on their own land and bankrupting countless companies with costly and unnecessary regulations and litigation.** Probably more than any other agency, the EPA is criticized for implementing disproportionately expensive regulations with little or no results.

- "U.S. environmental policy is out of control, costing jobs, depressing living standards and being run by politicians, scheming business people and social extremists" (Brimelow and Spencer, op. cit.).

- "[I]n a recent national survey of more than 200 corporate general counsels by *The National Law Journal* and Arthur Andersen Environmental Services, **only 30 percent of the attorneys said they believed that full compliance with all state and federal environmental laws is even possible.** Two-thirds said their companies had at some time in the past year violated some environmental regulation . . . The 1990 Clean Air Act will eventually produce 60,000 to 80,000 pages of regulations, requiring even a single company to collect millions of pieces of data on air emissions. 'Try arguing for 100 percent compliance with those kinds of numbers,' Frank Friedman, a Los Angeles attorney and the author of a textbook on corporate environmental management, told *National Law Journal.* Not every regulatory infraction entails a crime, but the complexity of the regulations makes inadvertent criminal conduct more likely" (R. Henderson, *Reason*, vol 25., no. 7, Dec. 1993, pp. 19-20).

Wetlands Policy: Enforcing the Indefinable

In recent years, the government has changed the definition of what constitutes wetlands, at the same time increasing its zeal and authority in protecting these areas. Author James Bovard provides a revealing look at the how the latest government policy regarding wetlands was created.

• "A few days after [President George] Bush was sworn in, EPA and the Army Corps of Engineers publicly released the Federal Manual for Identifying and Delineating Jurisdictional Wetlands, which contained a new definition of wetlands that repudiated the numerous preceding definitions of wetlands promulgated by federal agencies. The new manual was written in secret; **officials of several federal agencies met behind closed doors and effectively decided between themselves to claim jurisdiction over the property of hundreds of thousands of American landowners.** This was a stark violation of the Federal Administrative Procedures Act, which requires public notice and comment before a major Federal regulation acquires the force of law. Under the 1989 definition, land that was dry 350 days a year could be classified as a wetland. Even land that had no water on the surface could be classified as a 'Federal jurisdictional wetland.' [As] Robert J. Pierce, an Army Corps of Engineers official who helped to write the 1989 manual, later observed, '**Ecologically speaking, the term "wetland" has no meaning:** natural systems exist on a hydrologic gradient from ocean to desert. Somewhere in the middle are what society calls wetlands. **For regulatory purposes, a wetland is whatever we decide it is.** The type of natural systems that have been defined as wetlands has changed virtually every year for the last decade'" (Bovard, p. 34).

This change in the definition of wetlands dramatically increased the number of acres that now came under control of the EPA and the Army Corps of Engineers.

- "Based on dubious statutory authority, the EPA imposed wetlands rules requiring federal approval for even the most basic uses of an estimated 100 million acres of land, much of which is ordinarily dry . . . All told, as much as 5 percent of U.S. land, including **about 75 percent of Alaska and half of all farmland, arguably fell within Federal jurisdiction under the EPA's original regulations**" (Bandow, p. 5).

- "Fairness to Land Owners, a Maryland advocacy group, estimated that the new definition magically increased the amount of wetlands in the United States from roughly 100 million acres to up to 200 million acres. The vast majority of these new 'paper wetlands' were owned by private citizens" (Bovard, p. 34).

The EPA's and Army Corps of Engineers' enforcement of wetlands and Clean Water Act violations provides numerous examples of government run amok.

- "An elderly woman in Wyoming was prohibited by bureaucrats from planting a bed of roses on her land. A Pennsylvania couple was threatened with a Federal suit for installing a tennis court on their land. The charge was polluting a waterway. James and Mary Mills of Broad Channel, New York, were **fined $30,000 for building a deck on their house because, among other things, it cast a shadow on a wetland**" (Armey, *Freedom and Fairness Restoration Act,* pp. 25-26).

- "Landowners have been prosecuted or threatened with prosecution for removing trash, adding fill dirt, repairing a levee, installing a tennis court, plowing land, and planting crops without an Army Corps of Engineers permit. (John Pozsgai of Pennsylvania . . . is serving a three-year term for cleaning up a trash dump and then adding fill dirt to predominantly dry land ruled to be a wetland under the government's definition) . . . The law does little for conservation while violating people's rights to acquire and use their own property" (Bandow, p. 5).

- "Federal bureaucrats enforced the new [wetlands] definition with vengeance:

  Ronald Angelocci dumped several truckloads of dirt in the backyard of his Michigan home largely because a family member had acute asthma and allergies that were severely aggravated by the plants growing in the backyard. The Army Corps of Engineers decided to make an example out of Angelocci, launched a full-court offensive, and **had him jailed for violating the Clean Water Act. . . .**

Rep. James Hayes observed, "In Nevada, [housing] developments in the midst of cactus and parched earth are now being classified as 'wetlands' because standing water can occur for 7 days in a hole dug for a foundation. The fact that such a rain occurs very rarely no longer seems relevant in what was once considered a desert state, but which is now "The Great Wetlands State."" (ibid.).

- "The federal government once held up a license for a residential project in order to protect a 'wetland.' **The wetland in question was .0006 acres, or about the size of a ping pong table**" (Armey, op. cit., p. 23).

- "A Maryland couple, the Phillips, sold their house and spent their life savings to buy a 44-acre farm to use as their retirement home. They planned to pay for the purchase partly by selling a subdivision of the farm for development. But the Army Corps of Engineers declared it a wetland, barring all construction. No recompense was made" (ibid., p. 25).

- "Rich Savwoir, owner of the US 1 Auto Parts Store in Bethpage, New Jersey, faces a one-year prison term and a $10,000 fine because he didn't post a sign stating that his store accepts waste motor oil for recycling. Savwoir says that on the day in question the sign was down because a window-washer was working on the store" (Henderson, op. cit., p. 19).

- "A Louisiana family wanted to use eighty acres of land to build a crawfish pond and spent $35,000 to get the Federal permits. But at the last minute, the EPA denied permission because: 'High quality habitats such as these provide food, shelter, nesting and spawning areas to a wide variety of game and non-game fish . . . including the red swamp crawfish.' Rep. Billy Tauzin of Louisiana denounced the EPA for '**denying a permit to raise crawfish in an area they say should be used to raise crawfish**'" (Bovard, p. 35).

- "The U.S. government sent Bill Ellen, a Vietnam veteran and marine engineer, to prison for building duck ponds as part of a wildlife sanctuary on Maryland's Eastern Shore. Ellen began the construction of the wildlife sanctuary in 1988 after getting thirty eight government permits and having been advised by Army Corps of Engineers officials that the land was not classified as wetlands. In February 1989, armed with a new definition of wetlands, an Army Corps official reversed his position and arrived on the scene with a cease-and-desist order. Although Ellen ceased construction within forty-eight hours, the Army Corps still prosecuted him. Though environmental regulators tend to deify ducks, the Army Corps in this case claimed that Ellen was a polluter in part because the ponds he constructed attracted ducks, which generated waterfowl fecal matter. Ellen had created at least four times as many wetlands as he may have impaired, yet the U.S. government fought tooth-and-nail to send

Ellen to prison; a federal prosecutor demanded that 'those who commit criminal environmental insults [should] come to learn and appreciate the inside of a Federal correctional facility.' After the Army Corps had Ellen arrested, they dynamited his duck ponds to create a 400-yard channel connecting the land to a body of salt water—thereby destroying many of the environmental benefits from his project" (ibid., p. 36).

- "[E]nvironmental engineer Bill Ellen . . . served a six-month prison sentence for moving dirt. In 1987, Chicago commodities trader Paul Tudor Jones II hired Ellen, who had once regulated wetlands for the Virginia Marine Resources Commission, to build duck ponds on Tudor Farms—a $7-million development on 3,200 acres Jones owns in Dorchester County on Maryland's Eastern Shore. The development included fresh-water duck ponds . . . and enough crops and ground cover to attract migratory birds for hunters . . . Ellen argued that he followed environmental regulations to the letter, obtaining 38 separate development permits and hiring two former Maryland regulators who, when they had worked for the state, had helped draw maps that separated wetlands from uplands . . . [T]he Bush administration altered not only wetlands protection but also how wetlands were defined, adding millions of acres of private property to the nation's wetlands inventory. The new, broader definition increased the amount of wetlands in Dorchester County from 84,000 acres to more than 259,000 acres—and now included, regulators argued, Tudor Farms . . . On March 5, 1989, a Federal grand jury indicted Ellen . . . In May 1990 . . . Federal prosecutors charged Ellen with six counts of violating Section 404 of the Clean Water Act of 1972. Prosecutors claimed that Ellen had illegally altered a dozen acres of an 86-acre wetland; Ellen countered that he had obtained the permits to do that work, and had, in fact, created more than 50 acres of additional wetlands. So to convict Ellen, the government had to rely upon a technical violation: Ellen had defied a 'cease and desist' order and let workers move two truckloads of dirt from one spot on the property to another. According to the Federal wetlands manual, moving dirt can constitute illegally filling a wetland. In January 1991, a Baltimore jury convicted Ellen of five of the six counts" (Henderson, op. cit., p. 20).

Hazardous Waste or the Hazards of Waste?

Superfund and RCRA

Although hazardous materials cleanup would appear to be a worthwhile goal, the Environmental Protection Agency's enforcement of the Resource Conservation and Recovery Act (RCRA), a law passed in 1976 to regulate the treatment, storage, transport, and disposal of hazardous waste, and the Comprehensive Environmental Response, Compensation and Liability Act of 1980 (better known as **Superfund**) **has been a disaster. It also has been enormously expensive for the taxpayer.**

EPA has issued over 17,000 pages of regulations and proposed regulations on RCRA in the *Federal Register,* and EPA estimates that complying with RCRA costs businesses and governments an estimated $30 billion a year (Bovard, p. 73).

Since 1980, the federal government has spent almost $10 billion on Superfund and forced companies and private individuals to pay another $80 billion. **Despite costing a combined $90 billion however, "the program has cleaned up only 160 of the 1,202 most dangerous landfills and chemical dumps identified by the EPA"** (ibid., p. 70).

Estimates "of future expenditures under the Superfund program now range from $125 billion to a stupendous $1.25 trillion. Much of it—sometimes 85%—is going into transaction costs like lawyers' fees" (Brimelow and Spencer, op. cit.).

Examples of extravagance and regulatory excess under both RCRA and Superfund abound.

• "[U]nder the Environmental Protection Agency's hazardous waste disposal ban, only one premature death would be averted for each $4.2 billion of costs incurred . . . [T]hese same resources could be used to keep 47,890 dangerous criminals in prison for an additional three and one-half years" (John C. Shanahan and A. D. Thierer, Heritage Foundation *F.Y.I.* No. 11/94, Feb. 28, 1994, p. 3).

• "In 1986, Office of Management and Budget official Wendy Gramm criticized proposed RCRA regulations for presuming 'that the individual receives the maximum exposure to the substance—in effect that he would sink a straw into groundwater within the disposal facility property boundary and drank half a gallon of this [maximum-contaminated] water each day for 70 years'" (Bovard, p. 76).

• "[Former EPA Administrator William K.] Reilly has reportedly described [Superfund] as **the worst piece of legislation ever passed by the U.S. Congress**" (Brimelow and Spencer, op. cit.)

Example of an Endangered Business: Dry Cleaners

In 1993, the Environmental Protection Agency turned its attention to dry cleaners.

• "On July 15 [1993], the Environmental Protection Agency will issue new regulations on the use of dry cleaning's chief cleaning agent, dictating new operating procedures for dry cleaners and in many cases requiring the purchase of equipment that costs from $30,000 to $75,000 per machine . . . The new rules will necessitate new operating procedures and the purchase of equipment that retains perc [perchloroethylene] emissions and residue and recycles them for further use. The larger dry cleaners have 18 months to comply; the smaller shops have 36 months" (Chicago Tribune, July 4, 1993).

The new regulations wreaked havoc in an industry dominated by small business owners.

- "Environmental and other regulation can increase start-up costs for a single dry cleaner as much as $138,000 . . ." (Bovard, p. 72).

- "'By the end of 1993, **close to 15 percent of the dry cleaning industry will disappear,'** buckling under the weight of indebtedness, said William Seitz, executive director of the Neighborhood Cleaners Association, a national trade organization. 'Dry cleaners can't go into hock to make such (capital) improvements'" (*Chicago Tribune,* op. cit.).

- "The typical dry cleaning outlet is a small, family-owned business that grosses an average of $200,000 per year. Annual profits average in the neighborhood of $10,000. On average, each dry cleaner employs five people. When a business is this small, even seemingly minor requirements, such as spending an estimated 19 hours to fill out an EPA hazardous waste report, can have significant impact" (Jonathan H. Adler, *Washington Times,* Jan. 12, 1994).

Air Pollution and the B.B. (Bovine Belch) Factor

Air pollution is an important issue for the Environmental Protection Agency. Concern for such problems as acid rain drove Congress to enact sweeping changes in the law by passing the Clean Air Act amendments of 1990, which greatly expanded EPA's regulatory authority. The EPA also is pushing for higher standards for cars, lawnmowers, and other "polluters." Protecting the ozone and arresting global warming are so important to the agency that it is even **researching the impact of cow**

belches and flatulence on global warming. These activities, like others pursued by the EPA, are both costly and burdensome.

* "Government, business, and industry in our country spent approximately $115 billion for pollution control in 1990, and it is estimated that the figure will increase to $185 billion per year—that is 2.3 percent of our gross national product—by the year 2000. EPA continues to implement, I think, overly burdensome regulations while the Government continues to talk about creating jobs" (Sen. Frank H. Murkowski, R AK, *Congr. Record,* Mar. 10, 1994, p. S2677).

* "Remember the $300,000 study of whether cow flatulence contributes to global warming? Now the government's spending even more money to analyze what comes out of the front end of the cow. The Environmental Protection Agency has given Utah State University a $500,000 grant to round up rangeland cattle and fit them with special breathing devices that measure the amount of methane cows release when they burp. The new grant lets Utah State expand on a $300,000 study that began in 1991 at Washington State University and provoked widespread ridicule . . . Researchers estimate that confined cattle produce about 20 percent of global methane emissions. But two Cornell University economists concluded in 1991 that the methane emitted by one cow in a year has the same effect on global warming as the fuel burned to power a single 75-watt bulb" (*Chicago Tribune,* May 29, 1994).

- "[Driving to work] may soon be taken away from some of the 12.1 million commuters in 10 metropolitan areas subject to new Clean Air Act rules. Under a law kicking in this fall, any workplace of more than 100 people must develop ways to curb solo car trips . . . Penalties will vary from state to state because the Federal law gives state regulators wide latitude; in Texas, for example, employers can be fined $25,000 a day . . . '[T]his program gets some of the smallest emissions reductions at some of the highest costs,' says Al Giles, head of trip reduction at the Texas Natural Resource Conservation Commission. In Houston, trip reduction is expected to remove a scant 1.81 tons of pollutants from the air daily, 0.8% of the broader Clean Air Act goal of the city" (Caleb Solomon, *Wall Street Journal,* Sept. 8, 1994).

Lawnmowers and Other (Harmful?) Devices

At a press conference on May 4, 1994, the EPA announced that it was setting new emissions standards for lawnmowers and other gasoline-powered tools. "EPA Administrator Carol Browner, standing on the manicured lawn of the Washington Monument . . . said that the Federal government intends to impose unprecedented national emission standards on all new gas-powered garden tools sold in the United States." According to several news sources, the new emission standards also would cover such other gas-powered outdoor equipment as: chain saws, leaf blowers, golf carts, weed trimmers, pruners, generators, hedgeclippers, and soil cultivators.

The agency cited several reasons for its decision to regulate small engines.

- "The EPA said that 10 percent of air pollution in the U.S. is generated by 89 million pieces of lawn and garden equipment" (*Financial Post,* May 5, 1994).

- "The EPA estimates that the small engines spew 6 million tons of pollutants into the nation's air each year, or about 5 percent of air pollution. Running a mower for an hour creates as much pollution as driving a new car for 11 hours, the EPA said. One hour of using a leaf blower equals 34 hours of driving; for a chain saw, 63 hours of driving; for a weed trimmer, 21 hours" (Neil Bibler, *Associated Press,* May 5, 1994).

- "The primary fallacy . . . is **the assumption that we are in an air pollution crisis.** Although most Americans seem unaware of it, air quality in the United States has been improving steadily since about 1975 . . . In 1975, readings for carbon monoxide averaged 11.7 parts per million (ppm). In 1991 the average was 5.6 ppm, a decrease of 52 percent. This reading is also well below the Federal health standard of 9 ppm. The story is the same for ground-level ozone, which has fallen 25 percent since 1975 and has been within the Federal health standard since 1989 . . . Even if we take no action against lawn mowers, air quality will continue to improve, because of turnover in the automobile fleet and the phasing in of stricter industrial controls" (L. Howe, letter to editor, *Washington Post,* June 6, 1994).

Now that its lawnmower standards have been released, the EPA is eyeing other supposedly menacing products—like power boats and motorcycles.

- "EPA is developing the first national emission standards for gas-powered lawnmowers and garden equipment. And this fall, the Federal agency is expected to issue standards for marine engine emissions" (Cox News Service, *St. Petersburg Times,* May 25, 1994).

- "Motorcycles, boats and snowmobiles may be targeted later" (*USA Today,* May 5, 1994).

The Contaminant of the Week and Other Public Health Issues

A continuing fascination with public health issues has consumed the EPA and wasted billions of taxpayer dollars even though, according to *Forbes,* there has been "a little-publicized but dramatic shift in the public health field since the late 1970s. The Great Cancer Scare—which was used to shift the EPA's focus from 'bugs 'n' bunnies' to health—has been discredited. 'When looking at causes of cancer . . . pollution is almost irrelevant,' says Berkeley biochemist and cancer authority Bruce Ames" (Brimelow and Spencer, op. cit.).

It is therefore hardly surprising that another major criticism of the EPA is that **it focuses on potential health hazards without fully understanding the costs**

involved in tackling them and that this leads to the spending of incredible amounts of money on problems that may or may not have actual health consequences.

- "The cost per life theoretically saved—as measured by the EPA itself, often under statutory requirement—is now verging on the fantastic. 'I have never seen a single [proposed regulatory] rule where we weren't paying **at least $100 million per life** for some portion of the rule, or very few,' says Yale Law School Professor E. Donald Elliott, a Reilly ally and recent EPA general counsel. 'I saw rules costing $30 billion'" (ibid.).

The agency also is criticized for overreacting to substances like asbestos or dioxin: manipulating the scientific data to support its position, declaring widespread bans, and then discovering that the offending substances either were not as much of a threat to public safety as originally thought or that banning them actually increased the risk to public health.

- "EPA is now looking into the carcinogenic effects of taking showers" (John Shanahan, *Washington Times,* Dec. 6, 1992).

- "The result was a tangle of regulations that the Environmental Protection Agency estimates cost more than $140 billion a year, roughly $100 billion spent by industry and $40 billion by government. But what is now becoming apparent, some scientists and public health specialists say, is that some of these laws—written in reaction to popular concerns about toxic waste dumps or asbestos in the schools, as examples—were **based on little if any sound research** about the true nature of the threat . . . And with rare exceptions, Congress approved new laws without subjecting them to even rudimentary cost-benefit analyses" (Schneider, "New View Calls Environmental Policy Misguided").

- "People have a right to expect that public officials are making the right choices for the right reasons," says former EPA Administrator William K. Reilly. "We need to develop a new system for taking action on the environment that isn't based on responding to the nightly news. We're misallocating large amounts of money . . . What we have had in the United States is environmental agenda-setting by episodic panic" (ibid.).

- "Early in the 1980's, government scientists argued that exposure to asbestos could cause thousands of cancer deaths. Since asbestos was used as insulation in schools and public buildings, parents reacted with alarm. So in 1985 Congress approved a sweeping law that led cities and states to spend between $15 billion and $20 billion to remove asbestos from public buildings. But three years ago, the EPA completed research that prompted officials to admit that ripping out the asbestos had been **an expensive mistake;** the removal often sent tiny asbestos fibers into the air. Now, except in cases when the asbestos is damaged or crumbling, the government's official advice is: Don't touch it" (Schneider, op. cit.).

4

The Million-Dollar Menagerie
(Department of the Interior)

Introduction by John Shanahan

The Department of the Interior is responsible for protecting threatened animals and plants under the terms of the Endangered Species Act. Unfortunately, the administration of this law—like the administration of laws designed to protect the environment—all too often has been characterized by overzealousness and excess.

Most Americans have heard of the spotted owl controversy, with owls pitted against logging communities in the fight for survival. Unfortunately, however, Interior is doing little for either side. Instead, it uses the spotted owl and other threatened or endangered species as an excuse to lock up federal land so that only hikers may have access to it. But the agency does not stop there. The federal government owns almost four of every ten acres in the United States, but Interior has decided that more control is necessary. Thus, instead of being able to use their land as they see fit, **private landowners face possible jail time if they build a house or cut trees without Interior's prior approval**. When a landowner defaults on his mortgage because the income from his tree farm disappears, his "contribution" to preserving our natural heritage is little comfort.

Interior effectively confiscates the property of private citizens through regulation but **typically offers no compensation for the benefits it takes**. Like the EPA when it confiscates wetlands, Interior professes that it is merely pursuing a public good which the nation could not afford if it had to compensate landowners. But this superficial response ignores the fact that no public good can come from wronging private citizens. In its most basic sense, this is a question of fairness: Why should one American (or group of Americans) bear the entire burden of the government's pursuit of a national good? When Interior regulates, someone must pay; and if this regulation is truly for the public's benefit, then those who benefit should bear the costs.

Ironically, Interior actually is harming many threatened species. When threatened birds nest in the area with their young, for example, landowners outside the regulatory "zone" often clear-cut their property in self-protection. If one of the young birds nested in their trees, or even on nearby property, these landowners would lose millions in revenue because government consistently refuses to compensate them. As a result of this misguided policy, seas of viable habitat for threatened species become mere islands.

This chapter documents some of the problems presented by the administration of the Endangered Species Act, as well as real-life stories of the pain and suffering it has caused for those caught in the federal regulatory web.

A Large and Costly Regulatory Headache

The Endangered Species Act (ESA) became law in 1973 and must be reauthorized by Congress every five years. The Act "was designed to identify plants and animals [and fish] at risk of extinction and add them to a list of federally protected species. **Once a species has been listed, any use of the land inhabited by the species can be prohibited—'whatever the cost'**—until the species' condition has improved enough to take it off the list" (House Republican Conference *Issue Brief*, May 26, 1994, p. 5).

Like many other well intentioned Federal laws, the Endangered Species Act misses the mark. It is mired in perpetual and sometimes highly visible controversies (e.g., the imbroglio over the spotted owl); it causes hardships for private property owners, businesses, and developers; it confers enormous power on unaccountable bureaucrats; and it is costly to U.S. taxpayers.

• "Sold to Congress in 1973 as the only way to protect such rare creatures as the bald eagle and the manatee, the Endangered Species Act has become *a regulatory straitjacket* that mandates Herculean steps be taken to protect a total of 853 species, ranging from the Dudly Bluffs Bladder Pod to the Arkansas Fatmucket. Some 4,000 other plants and animals are official candidates for future listing" (*Wall Street Journal,* June 3, 1994, p. A14).

- "The Fish and Wildlife Service said that by 1997 the settlement would increase the number of endangered plants and animals afforded Federal protection to roughly 1,150 from 749 today [December 1992]. To reach that number, the Government will have to designate roughly 100 species a year for protection starting in the current fiscal year; that is double the rate at which it identified and provided safeguards for threatened species over the last 19 years" (K. Schneider, *New York Times,* Dec. 16, 1992, p. 192E).

- "As Ike Sugg, of the Competitive Enterprise Institute, wrote, 'perhaps that is why [Interior Secretary Bruce] Babbitt talks of **"discarding the concept of property** and trying to find a different understanding of natural landscape."' The Interior Secretary wants to do away with 'the individualistic view of property,' and adopt a more 'communitarian interpretation.' Mr. Sugg argues, 'in a world run by ecosystem managers, the right to private property would amount to the privilege to pay taxes'" (House Republican Conference *Issue Brief,* op. cit.).

- "Very quietly, the Clinton administration is seeking to ban recreational and economic activities—including hunting, fishing, swimming, canoeing, camping, picnicking, haying, forestry and farming—from the nation's 510 wildlife refuges. And while Congress has succeeded in forcing the postponement of this elitist policy, preservation ideologues within the White House continue to prepare the way for its eventual implementation" (Alston Chase, *Washington Times,* Sept. 15, 1994).

- "In one case, blunders by the Fish and Wildlife Service may have contributed to an extinction. The service spent nearly $3 million to buy Florida habitat for the endangered dusky seaside sparrow—and then neglected to manage the land properly. The last bird died in 1987" (Maura Dolan, *Los Angeles Times,* Dec. 22, 1994, p. A8).

- "About 2% of the species protected by the act received half of the federal and state funds spent on endangered species in fiscal 1990. Here are the 10 species that commanded the most government money in that year" (ibid.).

Species	Status	Expenditure
Northern spotted owl	Threatened	$9.7 million
Least Bell's vireo	Endangered	$9.1 million
Grizzly (brown) bear	Threatened	$5.9 million
Red-cockaded woodpecker	Endangered	$5.2 million
Florida panther	Endangered	$4.1 million
Desert tortoise	Threatened	$4.1 million
Bald eagle	Endangered	$3.5 million
Ocelot	Endangered	$3.0 million
Jaguarundi	Endangered	$2.9 million
American peregrine falcon	Endangered	$2.9 million

- "One of the Administration's most controversial moves is the establishment of the $160-million-plus National Biological Survey (NBS) to catalogue everything that walks, crawls, swims or flies around this country—on public and private lands. Critics of the program say **it will take years to complete, involve thousands of government scientists, and would clash with private property rights.** Secretary Babbitt has said as much in a speech to environmental writers: protection of the habitat 'is going to limit the ability of some landowners in some places to do anything they want.' An important wrinkle in the plan is that under the NBS, the Freedom of Information Act will be waived—meaning that property owners will not have access to the biological information gathered from their own property . . . As it stands, the National Biological Survey does not protect private property rights" (House Republican Conference *Issue Brief,* p. 7).

- "Northern California developer Richard Garlinghouse has had two projects in which he obtained an endangered species permit by setting aside land for the species. He estimated that the law raised his costs 1 percent to 5 percent. He recouped his costs by charging higher prices for the homes" (Dolan, op. cit., p. A8).

- "The 10 most expensive recovery plans for endangered species" (*Wall Street Journal,* June 3, 1994, p. A14):

Rank	Species	Cost
1.	Atlantic Green Turtle	$88.236 million
2.	Loggerhead Turtle	$85.947 million
3.	Blunt-Nosed Leopard Lizard	$70.252 million
4.	Kemp's Ridley Sea Turtle	$63.600 million
5.	Colorado Squawfish	$57.770 million
6.	Humpback Chub	$57.770 million
7.	Bonytail Chub	$57.770 million
8.	Razorback Sucker	$57.770 million
9.	Black-Capped Vireo	$53.538 million
10.	Swamp Pink	$29.026 million

Whatever Happened to Private Property Rights?

One of the most devastating consequences of the Endangered Species Act is that everyone from small property owners to major multinational corporations can be banned from using their land once an "endangered species" is sighted. Federal, state, and local bureaucrats can run roughshod over the rights of property owners exactly as they have done in cases involving wetlands and Superfund.

• "The Third Amendment . . . states that no soldier can 'be quartered in any home, without the consent of the owner.' Somehow, though, it apparently never occurred to the Founding Fathers that we might someday need an amendment against the arbitrary 'quartering' of endangered species on private land. Good thing the Founders didn't live to see the day, ours, when property owners all over America would be told to idle their land and effectively use it only as a wildlife refuge. Ambitious government 'ecosystem management' plans are **locking up millions of acres of private land—without compensation**" (*Wall Street Journal,* Apr. 19, 1994).

- "There also is no guarantee that a landowner who spends two years or longer getting a permit will not be required to go through the same process again if another animal on the property is listed. In many cases, large sums are spent just to figure out how to develop and comply with the act. One scientist described the law as **a kind of 'gravy train for consultants'**" (Dolan, p. A8).

- "On March 10, 1992, U.S. Fish and Wildlife Service and state agents trespassed fifteen miles onto Richard Smith's Texas ranch, accused him of poisoning eagles, and seized his pickup truck. The agents later tracked down Smith's seventy-five-year-old father, W. B. Smith, and seized his pickup truck—threatening to leave an old man who had had five heart bypass operations ten miles out of town with no transportation. The agents produced no evidence to support their accusation and returned the trucks nine months later without filing charges" (Bovard, p. 12).

The Well-Known Spotted Owl

By far the most famous and controversial "endangered species" is the spotted owl, which has become the centerpiece of the debate over the Endangered Species Act.

- "In the Pacific Northwest, [the government's] efforts to save the Spotted Owl have cost 30,000 jobs and reduced lumber harvests to 1.1 billion board feet a year from 5 billion. Since about one-third of lumber for home construction comes from the Northwest, the restrictions have sent the price of lumber skyrocketing. **The cost of building a 2,000-square-foot house has increased by at least $4,000 since 1992,** pricing at least 80,000 potential buyers out of the market" (*Wall Street Journal,* June 3, 1994, p. A14).

- "Consider that as U.S. timber production declines, demand for foreign timber escalates. Many countries will import more wood from nations such as Malaysia and Brazil, where forestry may be summarized by the cry 'TIMMM-BURRR!' Today, **Japanese firms are slicking off the lush Sarawak rain forest in Malaysia to feed a global wood market energized by U.S. logging bans**" (G. Easterbrook, *New Republic,* Mar. 28, 1994, p. 29).

- "Research is beginning to suggest that the spotted owl exists in numbers far greater than was assumed when the extinction alarm sounded. Whereas a headline-making 1986 Audubon Society report said that 1,500 spotted owl pairs throughout the United States was the number necessary to prevent extinction, it now seems that as many as 10,000 pairs may exist. 'It appears the spotted owl population is not in as bad a shape as imagined ten years ago, or even five years ago,' said David Wilcove, a biodiversity expert for the

Environmental Defense Fund. Thus Clinton's plan to shut down most Washington and Oregon logging may not only be unnecessary; it may be resting on an illusion" (ibid., pp. 22–23).

• "The Fish and Wildlife Service regularly prohibits timber harvesting on private property within 10,000 acres of owl nests. Perhaps most unfortunately, all of these job dislocations may be for naught. Although environmentalists maintain the Northern Spotted Owl needs old-growth forests, recent studies show the owl thrives in second growth forests as well. But damage has already been done. More than 15,000 logging and mill jobs have been lost since 1990, and tens of thousands more job losses are expected. Between October 1992 and April 1993, lumber prices have increased by 20 percent, amounting to an extra burden of between $10 and $12 billion on home buyers and renovators. By some estimates, these price increases add $4,600 to the purchase price of a typical single-family home" (House Republican Conference *Issue Brief,* op. cit.).

The Million-Dollar Kangaroo Rat

• "It is true, in Mr. [Michael] Rowe's case, that if he came up with $5,000 to hire a biologist he might be allowed the use of his land. If a biological survey found no K rats, then Mr. Rowe could earn the right to use his own land by paying the government $1,950 an acre in 'development mitigation fees'—to subsidize the purchase of occupied habitat elsewhere. The presence of a single rat, however, would negate even this limited option" (*Wall Street Journal*, Nov. 10, 1993).

- "Of $10 million spent by Riverside County officials to protect the rat, half has gone to attorneys, biologists and administrators" (Dolan, op. cit., p. A8).

- "Yshmael Garcia's Riverside, Calif., home was destroyed by brushfires last year after he was denied permission to clear brush near his home as a firebreak. The brushland in that county has been declared protected habitat of the endangered Stephens' kangaroo rat" (*Washington Times*, July 12, 1994, p. A6).

Other Expensive Critters

- "Marj and Roger Krueger spent $53,000 on a lot for their dream house in the Texas Hill Country. But they and other owners have been barred from building because the golden-cheeked warbler has been found in 'the canyons adjacent' to their land" (*Wall Street Journal*, Apr. 19, 1994).

- "Rep. Charles Taylor of North Carolina tells us of a farmer who found that a Red-Cockaded Woodpecker had moved on to his land . . . To protect it, he was required to suspend economic activity on 1,000 surrounding acres, costing him $1.8 million in profits. 'Now he is clear-cutting everything around it because if he doesn't, he fears the spread of the woodpecker will take up the total use of all his land,' says Rep. Taylor" (*Wall Street Journal*, June 3, 1994, p. A14).

- "Take the Iowa Pleistocene Snail. The author of its recovery plan notes that 'its major long-term cause of decline is cyclic climatic change.' In other words: the Ice Age ended. But 'with a return to glacial conditions it will be resuscitated over the major part of the upper Midwest, provided its relictual areas are preserved.' No time estimates are given" (ibid.).

- "With the listing of the California gnatcatcher in March [1993], more than 400,000 acres of Southern California coastal sage scrub were put off limits . . . Only 5% of the gnatcatcher's total habitat can be released for constructive use" (*Wall Street Journal,* Nov. 10, 1993).

- "Water-starved yards and dirty cars, the legacy of this year's drought, dramatize this growing community's need for a bigger water supply. But the federal government and a tiny freshwater clam are standing in the way. [Wilson, North Carolina's] plans for expansion of Buckhorn reservoir, where water levels are so low that rock islands and large grassy patches poke to the surface, are clashing with the endangered dwarf wedge mussel that dwells in Buckhorn's tributaries . . . The city . . . was counting on expansion of its reservoir . . . but [the U.S.] Fish and Wildlife [Service] said the project would have to be reconfigured to save the rare mussels" (*Associated Press,* Nov. 22, 1993).

- "In Travis County, TX, property values have dropped $359 million since the Fish and Wildlife Service listed the golden-cheeked warbler and the black-capped vireo as endangered. The State of Texas will lose $2 million in property taxes and the residents of the area are going to find it difficult, if not impossible, to sell their homes. An 80-year-old woman has been told to stop brush clearing her land. The government has warned her that failure to do so will subject her to fines of up to $50,000 and up to one year in prison" (Fields, "Introduction of the Property Owners Bill of Rights," p. E225).

5

Paying to Caesar What Is Caesar's?
(Internal Revenue Service)

Introduction

The Internal Revenue Service (IRS) is a 132-year-old institution that employs approximately 115,000 people to collect more than $1.12 trillion a year. Of all Federal bureaucracies, the IRS probably is known—and feared— by more Americans than any other.

- "The average American family head will be forced to do **20 years' labor** to pay taxes in his or her lifetime" (Bovard, p. 289).

- "It now takes you, the average taxpayer, about 11 hours to do your taxes. That adds up to 5.4 billion man-hours a year . . . for Americans to figure out how much they owe the IRS . . . According to *Forbes,* it's also **a $200 billion burden on the economy:** $100 billion spent filling out tax forms and another $100 billion wasted from 'investments made for tax rather than economic purposes'" (*Limbaugh Letter,* Sept. 1994, p. 14).

- "Today the average family of four pays **24.5 percent of its income** to the IRS (in 1950 it was 2 percent). Add in state and local taxes and the average family pays **40 percent of its income** to the government— more than it spends on food, clothing and shelter combined" (ibid.).

- "The Revenue Code of the United States, the law that is passed by Congress, is printed on some 2,200 pages. The I.R.S. regulations interpreting the law require an additional 7,600 pages. Last year [1988], *Money* magazine asked 50 tax preparers to complete the tax return of a hypothetical couple who earned a combined salary of $100,000 . . . **The 50 tax pros came up with 50 different tax bills.** When the magazine conducted the same survey with 50 other tax preparers this year, the confusion was even greater" (*New York Times Magazine,* Sept. 3, 1989).

- "*Money* magazine annually has a contest to test whether tax professionals can correctly ascertain a family's tax obligation in a relatively complex case; in 1993, **over 95% of tax experts gave the wrong answer.** If the experts cannot even correctly compute a person's tax obligation, then government officials end up with far more discretion to penalize people for giving wrong answers—even though the government officials themselves may not understand the law" (Bovard, p. 275).

Falling into the Hands of the IRS

With vast powers at its disposal, the IRS can make life miserable both for individuals and for businesses.

- "It's amazing how the IRS uses very similar tactics to organized crime. They both run their **operations based totally on fear** . . . If anyone speaks out against the IRS operation, it eats away at that fear. This is why they need to silence any critic who comes along, as it may erode their operation of fear" (*Freedom*, June 1990, p. 17).

- "Since 1954, the number of different penalties that the IRS can impose on taxpayers has increased over tenfold—from 13 to over 150. In 1992 the IRS imposed **over thirty-three million penalties** on taxpayers. The amount of penalties the IRS assesses has soared from a total of $1.3 billion in 1978 to $12.5 billion in 1992. The over one hundred new penalties created in recent decades amount to decks of trump cards the government can play against the citizen" (Bovard, p. 266).

- "Since 1980, the number of levies—IRS seizures of bank accounts and paychecks—has increased fourfold, reaching 3,253,000 in 1992. [The U.S. General Accounting Office] estimated in 1990 that the IRS imposes **over 50,000 incorrect or unjustified levies on citizens and businesses per year.** GAO estimated that almost 6 percent of IRS levies on business were incorrect" (ibid., p. 270).

- "The IRS also imposes almost one and a half million liens each year, an increase of over 200 percent since 1980. *Money* magazine conducted a survey in 1990 of 156 taxpayers who had IRS liens imposed on their property and found that 35 percent of the taxpayers had never received a thirty-day warning notice from the IRS of an intent to impose a lien and that some first learned of the liens when the magazine contacted them . . . **The worst credit stain a small business person can receive is an IRS lien**" (ibid., pp. 270-271).

- "To collect the information it deems necessary, the I.R.S. has the power to order—**without a warrant**—banks, employers and other institutions to provide data about a taxpayer. (All other Federal, state and local police forces are required to obtain a warrant to get such information.)" (*New York Times Magazine,* Sept. 3, 1989).

- "IRS agents make over 10,000 direct seizures of homes, cars, or pieces of property each year. The IRS has long rewarded its agents based on the amount of taxpayers' property they confiscate . . . IRS revenue officer Shirley Garcia told the Senate Finance Committee in 1987 that **IRS managers pressure employees to make more seizures** partly so that the managers can win 'merit pay' bonuses; the IRS personnel system used tax dollars to provide incentive bonuses for seizing taxpayers' property" (Bovard, p. 268).

- "*Money* magazine estimated in 1990 . . . that the IRS wrongfully collected up to $7 billion in penalties it assessed in 1989 but were not owed by taxpayers" (Bovard, p. 268).

Those Who Have Suffered

- "Two elderly women who ran a credit union for a Catholic church in Coopersville, Michigan, sent a letter to the IRS in 1985 requesting a waiver because they did not have a computer and had only fifty-nine form slips to file. The IRS never responded, and the credit union filed its tax return on paper. A year later, the IRS slapped a $2,950 penalty plus interest on the two women; when they refused to pay the bill, **the IRS imposed a lien on their checking account**" (Bovard, p. 267).

- "[A]rmed IRS agents seized Engleworld, an Allen Park, Michigan day care center . . . The seizure was carried out by the agency because Engleworld's owners owed the government more than $14,000 in back taxes, and has drawn fire from parents who maintain that they and their children were intimidated by IRS agents conducting the raid . . . 'It was like something out of a police state,' recalled Sue Stoia, one of the parents. Stoia had gone to Engleworld to pick up her seven-year-old daughter Catherine. Before they could leave with their children, parents say, they had to sign a form pledging to pay the government what they owed the day care center. 'They indicated you could not take your child out of the building until you had settled your debt with the school, and you did that by signing a form to pay the IRS,' Stoia explained. 'What we were facing was a hostage type situation. **They were using the children as collateral'**" (*Dollars & Sense,* Apr. 1985, p. 3).

- "In 1983, Rohm & Haas, a chemical manufacturer, sent the IRS a check for $4,448,112.88 for payroll taxes; **the IRS claimed the check was ten cents short and penalized the company $46,806.37.** The company assigned a team of accountants to the dispute and, after five months, the IRS dropped the penalty—but without explaining or apologizing for its action" (Bovard, p. 266).

- "Sen. David Pryor described a . . . case in 1987: 'A small businessman in El Dorado, Arkansas, filed over two hundred forms with the IRS. He then received a letter from the IRS informing him that he was subject to a $50 a form fine for not filling out the forms using a ten pitch typewriter. He called the IRS to let them know that his business only owned one typewriter and it was a 12 pitch. The agent told him to buy a new typewriter and pay the fines. The result of the IRS action: $10,000 in fines and $150 for a new typewriter'" (Bovard, p. 267).

• "In January 1993, the IRS burst into [Robert C.] MacElvain's Eufaula, Alabama, home and seized about 400 items, including his car, the family Bible and, his lawyer said, the diamond ring off his wife's finger. The IRS said MacElvain owed $2.2 million in back taxes, and the IRS was tired of fooling around. So was MacElvain. He countered by filing liens against the property of the IRS agent who led the seizure and the four local businessmen who helped. If any of them wanted to buy or sell something, or get a loan, they would have MacElvain's claim to contend with . . . The IRS was not amused. This has happened more than once, IRS sources said, and the agency is not interested in encouraging a trend. The government indicted MacElvain on eight counts of 'corruptly endeavoring to obstruct and impede the due administration of the Internal Revenue laws.' Last month [March 1994], a federal jury in Montgomery, Alabama, acquitted him on three counts but found him guilty on five others, including the liens on the four contractors. Now MacElvain is looking at three years in jail and a $250,000 fine, unless he can win an appeal" (*Washington Post,* Apr. 12, 1994).

In Danger: Independent Contractors

Businesses that use independent contractors are favorite targets of the IRS. The IRS inquisition into such businesses can be devastating in its effects and certainly makes companies less likely to employ independent outside vendors.

- "The IRS is carrying out **a campaign to slash the number of Americans permitted to be self-employed** and to severely punish the companies that pay them. Since 1988, the IRS's attack has devastated thousands of small businesses and is undermining high-tech industries, the healthcare industry, and even freedom of religion. The IRS is enforcing with a vengeance legal standards that even the U.S. Treasury Department admits are vague and unpredictable. The IRS's attack on the self-employed is an effort to fundamentally change millions of Americans' way of life—simply to make people more subjugated to tax collectors" (Bovard, p. 259).

- "The IRS has long sought to forcibly reduce the number of self-employed Americans and maximize the number subject to tax withholding. The IRS enforcement campaign is targeting businesses with less than $3 million in assets—in most cases, businesses without in-house counsel that cannot afford a lengthy court fight. The House Government Operations Committee concluded in a report in November [1992] that 'IRS' enforcement activities [on independent contractors] present small business taxpayers with **a veritable nightmare of problems and policies that defy common sense**'" (*Wall Street Journal,* Apr. 7, 1993, p. A14).

- "The IRS has long striven to minimize the number of self-employed. The General Accounting Office reported in 1977 that the IRS 'tends to classify as many persons as possible as employees, thereby subjecting their earnings to (tax) withholding.' . . . A 1992 House Government Operations Committee report observed, 'The IRS has a long-standing preference for employee designations rather than independent contractor designations. The IRS preference is due to the administrative convenience it produces for them (e.g., collection of taxes through withholding), the large back tax assessments that are calculated by using mandatory formulas when workers are reclassified, and a general assumption that employees are more compliant with the tax laws than independent contractors'" (Bovard, p. 260, 264).

- "Many IRS officials threaten harsh penalties to coerce businesses to sign agreements promising not to use independent contractors in return for a reduction or waiver of the taxes and penalties. Such perpetual cease-and-desist orders may be appropriate when the government is dealing with wife-beaters or child molesters, but they are bizarre when it is seeking a pretext to permanently control the day-to-day operation of small businesses" (*Wall Street Journal,* op. cit.).

- "IRS agents have assessed over $500 million in penalties and back taxes since 1988 (averaging $68,000 per company) and forced businesses to reclassify over 400,000 independent contractors as employees. (The IRS is now 'converting' almost 2,000 independent contractors into employees each week.)" (Ibid.)

- "The IRS estimates that there are 3.4 million Americans now working as independent contractors who should be reclassified as employees. The Small Business Administration estimates that there are roughly 5 million independent contractors nationwide. Thus, if the IRS achieves 'total compliance,' over half of all the current independent contractors in the United States could be forced to abandon their own businesses" (Bovard, p. 264).

Horror Stories Abound

- "John Bailey, a psychologist at the Family Therapy Center of Madison, Wisconsin, complained to a congressional committee in 1992 that his clinic 'has come under attack . . . The **IRS methods have been too subjective, applied with ferocity and arbitrariness,** and have caused untold grief for us and other well-meaning small businesses.' Bailey reported that the IRS 'attack has threatened the very survival' of several Wisconsin clinics. As part of its crackdown, IRS agents seized $2,000 out of the Center's bank account, and then, after being forced to concede that its case was baseless, claimed that it could not return the money because of difficulties with its computer system" (Bovard, p. 261).

- "Harvey Shulman, counsel for the National Association of Computer Consultant Businesses, observed: 'I have had grown men and women—40 or 50 years old—cry on the phone to me, telling me that their marriage is threatened, they are seeking counseling, all because the business that they built up in the last

15 years of their lives—the house and other things they've earned from the fruits of their labor—is all threatened by this IRS employment classification audit. They ask me, "What did I do wrong? Why am I being persecuted?"'" (*Wall Street Journal,* op. cit.).

* "IRS officials in some areas have ordained that all United Methodist ministers must be reclassified as employees. Rev. Robert McKibben of Alabama informed the House Ways and Means Committee that he was told by an IRS examiner that 'all ministers' are 'statutory employees.' . . . Craig Hoskins, counsel for the United Methodist Church, estimated that over a thousand Methodist clergymen have faced IRS audits over their employment status" (Bovard, p. 262).

Internal IRS Problems

Snoopers Get Caught

In the summer of 1993, the IRS disclosed that "368 employees in the Atlanta region were investigated in 1989 and 1990 for non-work-related monitoring of tax-payer files," or snooping. Senate Governmental Affairs Committee Chairman John Glenn (D-OH) reported that more than 1,300 IRS employees "have been investigated or disciplined for using government computers to browse through tax returns" and that "of the 1,300 employees nationwide that the IRS has investigated since 1989 more than 500 cases occurred in the last 10 months" (*Washington Post,* July 19, 1994).

- "All the employees investigated are suspected of mis-
using the IRS Integrated Data Retrieval System
(IDRS), which locates and adjusts taxpayer accounts.
Some 56,000 of the IRS' total 115,000 employees
(6,300 of 21,000 employees in the Southeast region)
have access to the system . . . The computer system is
notoriously outdated; the agency is several years
behind in audits. But the IRS is preparing for a $23-
billion computer overhaul, scheduled for completion
in 2008. The purpose of the modernization is to give
every employee who needs it on-line computer access
to taxpayer information as a way of improving cus-
tomer service . . . The IRS acknowledges **the system
will create more potential for abuse because more
IRS employees will have access**" (*St. Petersburg
Times*, Aug. 8, 1993).

- "In 154 [snooping] cases, employees were disciplined.
Deputy Commissioner Michael P. Dolan said three
employees were forced to resign, three were fired,
38 received suspensions, 67 were given reprimands,
24 were admonished, 17 underwent counseling and
two received 'caution letters'" (*Washington Post*,
Aug. 5, 1993).

Bad Bookkeeping

The IRS conveniently does not hold itself to the same
rigid standards that it forces taxpayers to follow.

- "The taxpayer who can't find a lost receipt to justify a
deductible expense might take some solace in the way

the IRS dealt with a missing contract: It paid $36,000 for maintenance on a computer that had not been used for three years. And what of the taxpayer wondering whether the clothes he donated to Goodwill are really worth a $300 deduction? The IRS, according to federal auditors, valued one of its $13,000 printers at more than $5 million. It bought two pieces of computer equipment at $6 million each and claimed that they were worth $11.8 million each . . . Can't pay your taxes on time? In a random sample of 280 IRS payments to vendors, GAO auditors found that 81 were made after the due date" (Swanson, "IRS Books an Auditor's Nightmare").

- "The Internal Revenue Service, which demands that taxpayers be able to produce records to back up all claims of income and deductions, could not live up to that standard itself, according to a study released . . . by Congress's General Accounting Office. In its report, the second annual examination of the IRS's financial statements, the GAO was 'unable to express an opinion on the reliability' of what the agency said because of missing records, 'ineffective internal controls and unreliable information'" (*Houston Chronicle*, June 17, 1994).

General Misconduct

- "[O]ne revenue officer in Philadelphia laughed about the time he told a delinquent mother who had no income and no other means of payment that 'If you can't pay your taxes, then bring your kids in and we'll sell them for you.' In Virginia, supervisors used to tell stories about how the Chief of Collections rose through the ranks. It was alleged, for instance, that as a revenue officer, the Chief had a detachable red blinking light and a siren that he would turn on as he pulled into a taxpayer's driveway. It was also alleged that the Chief once seized a car while it was in a funeral procession . . . One [Virginia] supervisor used to walk through his group daily repeating 'levy and seize,' over and over again. . . " (*Tax Savings Report,* June 1989).

- "The IRS imposes almost no controls over its own agents' property seizures. GAO reported in September 1992 that each agent was practically on the 'honor system' to officially report and account for property he seized from taxpayers . . . [Y]et if the property 'disappears' after an IRS seizure, the agency refuses to credit the taxpayer whose property was looted . . . GAO found that among the items seized by IRS agents which were later stolen were 'televisions, VCRs, telephones, and scuba equipment in Atlanta; $10,000 in groceries from a seized market in Miami; and a 1980 gold Krugerrand in Phoenix'" (Bovard, pp. 269–270).

6

The Over-Regulated Workplace
(Occupational Safety and Health Administration)

Introduction by Susan M. Eckerly

The Occupational Safety and Health Administration (OSHA) was established in 1970 by the Occupational Safety and Health Act in order to protect worker safety and health. As the stories that follow demonstrate, however, the agency's effectiveness in carrying out its mission is **being called into question by both organized labor and the employer community.**

With an annual budget of some $300 million, the agency is charged with enforcing safety and health regulations at over six million worksites. The 1970 Act established a joint Federal-state approach, authorizing states to run their own programs. Twenty-one states run their own safety and health programs, which are supervised by Federal OSHA and which must be "at least as effective" as the Federal program.

Although the number of workplace deaths has declined since the Occupational Safety and Health Act was enacted, critics question its overall effectiveness. For too long, the agency has focused on the size of its inspector force, the number of inspections, and the size of the penalties instead of on whether or not it was addressing the most serious hazards in the workplace. For example, about one-third of the 6,083 work-related deaths in 1992 were caused by motor vehicle accidents and workplace violence—two areas not regulated by the agency.

From the early days of the agency, complaints about OSHA also have focused on the fact that the agency's rules and enforcement activities are **cumbersome and heavy-handed.** OSHA health and safety regulations often have taken years to implement because of court challenges. One rule dealing with locking out equipment not in use took over ten years to implement. Another rule, the hazard communication standard which requires hazardous chemicals to be labeled, is criticized frequently by employers because of its burdensome paperwork requirement.

Another area of concern is **enforcement.** The agency currently spends three times as much on enforcement as it does on helping employers comply with rules. Currently, more than half of the violations cited by OSHA are **paperwork violations.**

Two popular compliance programs, the Voluntary Protection Program and the on-site consultation program, suffer from lack of funding. Both programs are popular with employers because they concentrate on helping employers comply with the rules rather than on imposing penalties.

Agency reform efforts have focused largely on two different approaches. One so-called reform effort introduced in the past two Congresses seeks to make the agency more effective by increasing its funding levels, mandating new regulations, and boosting agency enforcement efforts by such things as creating new criminal penalties. The Clinton Administration endorsed this position despite a different approach advocated in Vice President Gore's National Performance Review. Recognizing the budgetary constraints that will continue to face the agency, Gore endorsed coming up with different approaches, such as having the agency set standards and requiring certification by independent auditors.

The other approach, introduced in the last Congress and in 1995, seeks to ensure a safe workplace, but in the most effective and least burdensome way. It would change the agency's penalty structure to eliminate minor ones. This reform effort generally would give more funding to compliance programs like the Voluntary Protection Program than to enforcement. Not unlike Vice President Gore's suggestion, this approach seeks to offer employers the incentive to provide a safe workplace.

- "In the wide-ranging [National Association of Manufacturers] survey, business owners said that OSHA regulations and product liability laws were among the issues that particularly worried them" (Bureau of National Affairs *Daily Labor Report,* Apr. 29, 1993).

- "The [Clinton] administration has announced its support for **a workplace safety bill estimated to cost companies more than $50 billion a year.** It would require companies to, among other things, establish comprehensive safety programs, safety committees and so forth. Labor Secretary Robert Reich went even further, saying in a draft letter to Sen. Edward Kennedy, D-Mass., and Rep. William Ford, D-Mich.—sponsors of the bill—that he would move administratively to 'require all employers to establish comprehensive occupational safety and health programs,' and to have these programs 'regularly certified'" (*Investor's Business Daily,* Apr. 19, 1994).

- "Under new rules expected to affect 240,000 work sites and 1.6 million workers, the Occupational Safety and Health Administration is ordering companies to clearly mark and limit access to confined spaces. The rules are expected to prevent 54 deaths and more than 5,000 serious injuries a year, OSHA said. **Compliance is expected to cost companies $202.4 million a year . . .** By definition, confined spaces are big enough for employee entry, have limited means of access and aren't designed for continuous employee occupancy" (*Wall Street Journal,* Jan. 14, 1993).

- "In Florida, the owner of a three-person silk-screening company was fined by OSHA—the Occupational Safety and Health Administration—for not having a Hazardous Communications program for his two part-time employees" (Oliver, "How to Think About Regulations," p. 9).

- "The Chicago *Sun-Times* tells the tale of Robyn Lerman of Highland Park, Illinois, a 6-year-old who recently lost her first teeth. Because the two baby biters weren't coming out on their own, Robyn's mother, Debbie, decided to let a professional force the issue. But when dentist Barry Karlov finished removing the teeth, he refused to hand them over to the child, who wanted to leave them under her pillow and get some compensation from the Tooth Fairy. It's not that Karlov is a bad guy; the government will not let him give Robyn her teeth. According to the *Sun-Times,* guidelines established this year [1992] by the Occupational Safety and Health Administration require that human tissues, including teeth, be immediately placed in an enclosed container for disposal. 'To say it's a sign of the times is an understatement,' Karlov told the paper. 'It's downright goofy is what it is. The Federal government can't get rid of Saddam Hussein, but here they are trying to put the Tooth Fairy out of business'" (*Insight,* Oct. 18, 1992, p. 19).

- "[T]wo employees of DeBest Inc., a plumbing company, were working at a construction site in Garden City, Idaho, when they heard a backhoe operator yell for help. They ran over, and found that the wall of a trench—which was NOT dug by DeBest—had collapsed on a worker, pinning him under dirt and covering his head. 'We could hear muffled screams.' said one of the DeBest employees. So the men jumped into the trench and dug the victim out, quite possibly saving his life . . . What OSHA did . . . was FINE DeBest Inc. $7,875. Yes. OSHA said that the two men should not have gone into the trench without (1) putting on approved hard hats, and (2) taking steps to ensure that other trench walls did not collapse, and water did not seep in. Of course this might have resulted in some discomfort for the suffocating victim ('Hang in there! We should have the OSHA trench-seepage-prevention guidelines here within hours!')." (Barry, "Federal agencies still waste deep in safety silliness").

• "The deep alienation felt by small business is exemplified in how they view their government. By a 2-to-1 margin, both owners and employees of small business viewed the government as an opponent rather than a partner in their pursuit of the American dream. Both owners and employees felt that the government is 'far too large and has far too much power'—82 percent of owners and 72 percent of employees agreed with this statement . . . From 1989 to 1992 alone, the regulatory burden on small business increased over 34 percent, amounting to $130 billion more in costs. Since 1992, new regulations have added untold billions. The distinguished oppressor of small business (next to the Internal Revenue Service) is the Occupational Safety and Health Administration (OSHA). It imposes unfathomable regulatory requirements, without regard for cost or efficacy, along with considerable paperwork burdens. And OSHA has the unchecked power to enforce all of the preceding. **Most remarkably, studies show that for all its pains and burdens, OSHA had no measurable impact on workplace injuries. Incredibly, 70 percent of the employees surveyed think 'there are too many workplace regulations and government should mind its own business'"** (*Washington Times,* Dec. 8, 1994, p. A23).

• "OSHA and EPA have taken the first fledgling steps toward coordinated enforcement. Is industry headed for better—or just more—regulation? Suppose you're responsible for occupational safety or environmental protection at a major petrochemical facility. Perhaps you've never been through a full-fledged OSHA inspection, but one day, without warning, nine government inspectors (seven from OSHA and two from EPA) show up at your plant. At a joint opening conference, OSHA and EPA team leaders explain that your plant has been targeted for a comprehensive inspection under OSHA's special emphasis program for the petrochemical industry (PetroSEP). During the next several weeks, OSHA compliance officers review your programs for chemical process safety, hazard communication, lockout/tagout, respiratory protection and so on. Meanwhile, EPA inspectors conduct a multimedia inspection examining air and water quality, toxic substances, and solid waste. Occasionally, the OSHA and EPA inspectors meet to discuss their findings and exchange information. The EPA inspectors are on your site for two weeks. OSHA officials are there for four months. Finally, when all the inspectors are gone, you have to wonder, 'What hit me?' You've just experienced what can happen, and is happening, when OSHA and EPA team up. In the last year or so, the two agencies have been doing joint inspections, conducting joint studies, referring potential violations to each other, coordinating standards work, exchanging reporting data, and developing cross-training for each other's staff. So far, the effort is limited and mostly symbolic, not much more than a few pilot projects, but government officials say it's an idea with far-reaching potential" (*Occupational Hazards,* Mar. 1992, p. 43).

• "Today, many employers complain that health and safety standards issued by the Occupational Safety and Health Administration (OSHA) are so voluminous, complicated and incoherent that they are not understandable to the average employer. This criticism raises a fundamental constitutional question: Do our constitutional principles allow OSHA to hold ordinary, well-meaning employers civilly and criminally liable for violating standards that they cannot understand? . . . While it is settled law that a vague

OSHA standard is unconstitutional, in practice it has been difficult (but not impossible) for employers to prove. The Federal courts have required employers to prove that a standard was vague as it was applied to the specific circumstances of the employer. Thus, each determination of vagueness turns on the specific facts of the case at hand. This judicial approach is a double-edged sword. While it makes it difficult for employers to prevail, just because an OSHA standard has survived a vagueness challenge is no guarantee that it will survive future challenges under different facts . . . Undoubtedly, as employer frustration with the lack of clarity and the complexity of OSHA health and safety standards continues to increase, the number and types of constitutional challenges also will increase. OSHA could avoid these challenges altogether by simply writing standards that are clear and easily understood by the average employer" (*Occupational Hazards,* Nov. 1993, p. 65).

• "The Occupational Safety and Health Administration (OSHA) has existed for 20 years. During the past 10 years, however, the budgeting for inspections has been progressively squeezed. Consequently, the number of inspections has declined annually since 1985. Dairy processors may feel that fewer inspections resulted in less time spent inspecting and therefore reduced penalties. Instead, OSHA has reacted to its limited ability to conduct inspections by more 'discoveries' of serious violations and by assessing greater penalties for those violations. In 1983, OSHA cited employers for only one serious violation in every three inspections. By 1992, the agency averaged at least two serious violations for every inspection; a six-fold increase. The cost of penalties is even worse. The average 'proposed' penalty has increased tenfold since 1983. In that year, the total proposed penalties were approximately $4 million. By 1992, penalties exceeded $40,000,000. Aggravating the situation are maximum penalties that have increased seven times so that each serious violation can now carry a penalty of $7,000. In addition, interpretations of violations are becoming more stringent. For example, OSHA inspectors are now citing each missing entry in a workplace injury log as a separate serious violation, instead of a single violation for a poorly maintained log. In this situation, an employer could be subject to a $7,000 penalty for each missing entry. Over a year, this could add up to an extreme amount of money if not watched closely" (*Dairy Foods,* Jan. 1994, p. 58).

7

Feel-Good Regulation
(Disability and Affirmative Action)

Introduction by Adam D. Thierer

The "Americans with Disabilities Act" (ADA) is an example of 'feel good' law—legislation that appeases a legislator's sense that it is their duty to right all wrongs. Yet, policy makers now must realize that their good intentions have had disastrous results.

When Congress was debating passage of the ADA, few legislators questioned its egalitarian intent to accommodate persons with disabilities throughout society. Unfortunately, fewer policy makers stopped to ask **if this goal was even achievable and what would be the costs the law would impose on society as a whole.**

As a result, the ADA has become a legal wrecking ball that allows lawyers to sue any establishment in America with the hope of destroying those businesses and confiscating their profits. This chapter documents this litigious and destructive nightmare. Good intentions have meant the loss of millions of dollars for small and big business alike and a corresponding loss of employment opportunities in those companies. **Worst yet, those recovering the rewards from ADA cases are often not "disabled" at all.** They are simply opportunistic parasites who live off the profits and hard work of others.

The ADA and the agency that enforces these regulations, the Equal Employment Opportunity Commission (EEOC), prove that two wrongs never make a right. For years the EEOC has terrorized American businesses with threats of federal lawsuits for not meeting race-based quota requirements. Now, the EEOC uses its newest weapon of choice — the ADA — to destroy companies and discourage entreprenuership. As a result, the EEOC and the federal laws that they enforce like the ADA, are **destroying the very job-creating opportunities that could put persons with disabilities or disadvantages to work.** In addition, the onslaught of ADA lawsuits has led to a bureaucratic backlog of casework that EEOC officials cannot grapple with.

Any legislator, regulator, or average American who reads this chapter will be forced to admit that the costs of the ADA clearly exceed its few benefits. Unfortunately, the failed economics of good intentions are likely to prevail and the ADA will remain on the books for many years to come. But as this chapter proves, often the most noble-minded laws have the most destructive effect upon the American economy, with little to show in the way of benefits.

Overview

In 1990, Congress passed the Americans With Disabilities Act—sweeping civil rights legislation for the handicapped. While the goal of protecting the rights of the handicapped seems unexceptionable on its face, however, its actual implementation has proved excessively burdensome, and the **magnitude of its economic consequences** for American business is only beginning to become apparent.

- "All over the U.S., businesses have spent millions of dollars to send their managers to seminars and speeches to learn how to comply with the ADA. But instead of receiving enlightenment, those managers often return to their businesses with their heads spinning. Troubled by the cost of compliance, and confused over the scope of the new edicts, many of those affected by the law have made a business decision to wait to be sued, rather than to comply voluntarily ... The list of required reading to understand the ADA is daunting even to experienced attorneys and ensures that virtually no lay employer can ever fully come to grips with the law—let alone fully comply with it. The problems only begin with the definition of 'disability,' which casts so wide a net that it includes even allergies and learning problems. And because disabilities are self-identified by the employee under the ADA, that means that the accommodations required of the employer are also defined by the employee . . . **[P]ast drug abuse is considered a 'disability' within the protection of the ADA. To add to confusion, current addiction to legal drugs or alcohol is also protected under the ADA . . .**" (*Wall Street Journal,* March 15, 1993, p. A12).

ADA and EEOC Horror Stories

- "The ADA increases the power of federal bureaucrats and lawyers over normal, law-abiding American businesses . . . In the first thirteen months of the law's operation, the EEOC [Equal Employment Opportunity Commission] received **over 13,000 allegations** of illegal discrimination against the disabled" (Bovard, p. 186).

- "The ADA has estimated **compliance costs of $100 billion over a five-year period**, the report [released on November 7, 1992, by Representative Richard K. Armey of Texas] says, in addition to 'tens of billions of dollars' a year arising from expected litigation under the ADA. The law is expected to be more burdensome on small business since hiring choices 'made to satisfy criteria other than those of economic efficiency have greater potential for creating adverse productivity effects on small businesses than on large,' the report said" ("Legislative Mandates Stifling Job Creation for Small Firms," op. cit.).

- "Look at the Americans with Disabilities Act. That is **a gold mine for bureaucrats** writing the regulations required or desired, and lawyers looking for fees love it—Americans fail in front of it. As I found out several days ago, small communities in my state [Wyoming] cannot or are not even allowed to resurface a road because it requires curb ramps to be installed simultaneously" (Speech by Malcolm Wallop, R-WY, in *Congr. Record,* May 2, 1994, p. S4942).

- "TCF Bank Savings of Minneapolis . . . is not sure what qualifies, in the words of the disabilities act, as 'reasonable accommodations' that are 'readily achievable' and don't cause 'undue hardship' for a business. So it's trying to cover all potential points of contention. One such effort is the installation of Braille instructions on drive-up automated teller machines . . . 'We made the point [in discussing the change] there were **no blind people driving up to our ATMs,**' says TCF Chairman William Cooper" (*Insight,* Jan. 24, 1993, p. 18).

- "According to the EEOC, the larger a person's waistline becomes, the more legal rights he acquires. The EEOC announced in August 1993 that obesity should be regarded as a 'protected' disability under the Americans with Disabilities Act . . . This ruling potentially **adds millions of people to the classes 'protected' by the ADA**" (Bovard, p. 187).

- "The ADA requires that in some cases, businesses must hire people to work as readers, interpreters, or travel attendants to accommodate the needs of disabled employees. When the EEOC first announced its regulations on this in July 1991, disabled groups were outraged that the federal government had not also required businesses to provide toilet assistants to the handicapped as a 'reasonable accommodation' to achieve equal opportunity with other workers . . . Chris Bell, EEOC assistant legal counsel, observed in 1991, 'Whether or not **a personal assistant would be required** for toileting and eating is going to have to be determined on a case by case basis. We didn't rule it out . . . It may be in some circumstances that will be required'" (Bovard, pp. 187–188).

8

Miscellaneous Madness
(Housing and Homelessness)

During the summer of 1994, the U.S. Department of Housing and Urban Development (HUD) became embroiled in a major controversy over whether a Berkeley, California, motel should be converted into housing for the homeless. The issue was not homelessness, however, but HUD's handling of those who objected to the project. The result: **"a national outcry erupted over [HUD's] investigation of three Berkeley, California, residents** who had peacefully protested the siting of homeless housing in their neighborhood."

- "In recent weeks, the heavy-handed HUD campaign in Berkeley has drawn embarrassing publicity. HUD demanded that the three protesters turn over all files, minutes of neighborhood meetings and everything written about the project. And HUD is accused of offering to end the intimidation if the three would just shut up" (*U.S. News & World Report,* Aug. 29, 1994, p. 20).

- "According to HUD officials, organized opposition to homeless shelters and other social-service facilities—if it is based on the attributes of the people involved—enjoys no First Amendment protection. Such opposition, says HUD, violates the Fair Housing Act Amendments of 1988, which are supposed to safeguard the housing rights of the disabled. **HUD and the Federal courts have defined addiction and alcoholism, as well as AIDS and mental illness, as Federally protected disabilities**" (*Wall Street Journal,* Sept. 14, 1994, p. A19).

- "The Berkeley Three are free. Joseph Deringer, Alexandra White and Richard Graham went up against the modern police state and won. The Department of Housing and Urban Development last week dropped a seven-month investigation against the trio, who had fallen under the evil eye of HUD after voicing opposition to a housing project for the homeless that is planned near their homes. The HUD vigilantes launched their investigation under the terms of the Fair Housing Act, which protects the housing rights of, among others, the mentally ill and people with drug or alcohol problems. Many of the homeless fall into either or both categories, and according to the imaginative definition of the HUD thought police, opposition to housing proposals based on such attributes as mental illness or substance abuse constitutes harassment and is not protected by the First Amendment. . . . [H]ow did the Berkeley Three ever get charged in the first place? **For saying what they thought, they faced fines of up to $100,000 and a year in jail**" (*Wall Street Journal,* Aug. 8, 1994).

- "The Berkeley Three are not an isolated example of HUD's outreach. Across the country, HUD's thought police have silenced critics with fines and threats" (ibid.).

- "The Department of Housing and Urban Development is threatening and investigating private citizens who oppose publicly financed housing projects in their communities—even though their opposition is in the form of letters, public statements and lawsuits. . . . **[HUD] is increasingly targeting individuals and community groups** that oppose proposed projects neighboring their homes. Seattle lawyer Roger M. Leed said he's represented two groups 'formally investigated by HUD' for writing letters, appearing at hearings or filing court actions against federally subsi[di]zed housing projects in their neighborhoods for people with mental disorders or histories of substance abuse or other 'disabilities'" (*Washington Times,* Aug. 8, 1994).

Business and Labor Practices

- "In New Jersey's suburban Bergen County, the county government issued **18 pages of regulations for the shoe-shine stand in the lobby of the county court-**

house. The new rules subjected the concession to a competitive bidding, and the operator to a dress code—a dark brown or burgundy knee-length wraparound smock, with pockets. Robert Taylor, who has operated the stand for the past 12 years without benefit of official guidelines, wears a sleeveless apron, doesn't have the required cash register, or a $1 million insurance policy. The saga came to an end after the matter gained coverage in the *New York Times* and the *Wall Street Journal.* The county rewrote a simpler version of the law" (Americans for Tax Reform Foundation, "Cost of Government Day 1994," p. 8).

• "Postal clerk Joannie McCaughey, an 11-year veteran of the U.S. Postal Service, was chagrined when she received a disciplinary letter from a supervisor for the Cambridge, Massachusetts, facility where she works. 'This practice must stop immediately,' the letter warned. 'Future deficiencies . . . will result in more severe disciplinary action being taken against you, including suspension or removal from the Postal Service.' Ms. McCaughey's infraction: On August 9, she had punched the time clock at 8:59 a.m.—one minute before her shift was scheduled to start. Three other postal workers received similar letters. . . . Michael Hannon, the supervisor, says, 'I don't think I made a mistake.' He adds that **if every employee wanted to punch in one minute early every day, 'it would become an abusive situation'**" (*Wall Street Journal,* Oct. 4, 1994).

National Forests

- "Underage drinking, swearing, playing loud music,
  target shooting and rock hunting could get you in
  trouble under regulations being considered for the
  country's national forests. . . . A copy of the new
  Forest Service rules can be found in the Federal Register, Volume 59, No. 32. . . . There are dozens of pro-
  hibitions in the 12 pages of regulations, including laws
  that make it a Federal class B misdemeanor to:

  "Use obscene language or gestures 'with intent
  to cause public alarm.'

  "Make an 'unreasonably loud noise.'

  "Operate a radio, television or musical instru-
  ment in or near a campfire or adjacent to a body
  of water.

  "Not wear a seat belt when driving within a
  forest" (*Rapid City Journal,* Apr. 10, 1994,
  p. A1).

Banking

- "Chevy Chase, a prosperous Maryland thrift . . . ,
  recently found itself accused by the U.S. Injustice
  Department of discriminating against blacks. The
  Injustice Department claimed that Chevy Chase dis-
  criminated against blacks because it did not open
  enough branches in 'majority African-American cen-
  sus tracts' in the District [of Columbia] and Prince
  George's County. Even though bank regulators had

denied Chevy Chase's attempts to expand beyond its suburban base into D.C. in the late 1980s, the Injustice Department found the bank **guilty of a crime so new that it is not even on the statute books**—an insufficient number of D.C. branches and failure to aggressively market loans to blacks. . . . Chevy Chase is being forced . . . to open three mortgage offices in 'majority African-American neighborhoods in D.C.,' to open a branch bank in Anacostia (the area that puts the District of Columbia in the record books for drug-related murders), and to open other new branches in other black neighborhoods. In addition, the bank must provide more than $11 million in below-market loans to blacks with interest rates 'at either 1 percent less than the prevailing rate or 1/2 percent below the market rate combined with a grant to be applied to the down-payment requirements.' . . . Clinton's Injustice Department has imposed an unprecedented quota straitjacket on Chevy Chase, mandating black employees at all levels of its operation, advertisements in black publications and radio stations, marketing outreaches to black real estate agents, and racial quotas on loan sales calls and advertising models. To top it all off, Chevy Chase must subject its personnel to Orwellian 'sensitivity' and 'diversity' indoctrination seminars to guarantee that employees deliver the mandated special privileges to blacks" (Washington Times, Sept. 1, 1994, p. A16).

Please Join The Heritage Foundation

For only $15 you can become a member of the most influential conservative think tank in America. You'll receive a quarterly newsletter, a handsome membership card, and surveys that tell Congress what you think on important issues facing America. Your contribution will help Heritage's fight to role back big government and get rid of the red tape that is strangling America.

Or Join Heritage's CongressWatchers

For your $100 contribution you become a member of the Heritage CongressWatchers. You'll receive a free copy of every Heritage publication about Congressional reform and term limits, in addition to all the benefits of Heritage membership.

THE HERITAGE FOUNDATION
214 Massachusetts Ave., N.E.
Washington, DC 20002

☐ Yes. I want to become a member of The Heritage Foundation and help in the fight to roll back big government and get rid of red tape.

I've chosen the following membership option:

☐ $15 membership fee

☐ $100 to join the Heritage CongressWatchers Club
Please send me your latest Heritage report on Congress.

Enclosed is my check for $_____

Name _____

Address _____

City _____ St. _____ Zip _____